MARK SHIELDS
On the Campaign Trail

MARK SHIELDS
On the Campaign Trail

*Wise and witty dispatches from the front
lines of the 1984 Presidential race*

*with cartoons by ten of the nation's
leading political cartoonists*

Algonquin Books of Chapel Hill
1985

Algonquin Books of Chapel Hill
Post Office Box 2225
Chapel Hill, North Carolina, 27515-2225

LIBRARY OF CONGRESS CATALOGING IN PUBLICATION DATA
Shields, Mark.
On the campaign trail.
1. Presidents—United States—Election—1984—Addresses, essays, lectures. 2. United States—Politics and government—1981– —Addresses, essays, lectures.
I. Title
E879.S55 1985 324.973'0927 85-1301

ISBN 0-912697-22-9
ISBN 0-912697-21-0 (pbk.)

Introduction

*I*f there is a single premise (a premise is what some of us like to call our prejudices) upon which this slim volume rests, it is this writer's abiding affection for American politics and politicians. Politics—which is nothing less than the peaceable resolution of conflict among legitimate, competing interests—is an important public occupation and it ought to be respected. That the practice of politics is not uniformly esteemed in our nation can be mostly ascribed to the practices of politicians, in whose roguish company I have been lucky enough to spend most of the past twenty years.

The election year of 1984 was even more special than most. I was able to cover the presidential campaign from before the frostbite in New Hampshire to the sunburn in California, the San Francisco Democratic convention and the Republican convention in Dallas, and the fall campaign right up to and through election day. It was a fascinating time during which I wrote a lot of words for my five-times-a-week radio reports "On the Campaign Trail" and for my twice-a-week column for the *Washington Post* and, as they say, "other fine newspapers."

As most people who follow politics at all are probably aware, political writers are addicted to prediction-making the way many civilians are addicted to cashews—i.e., once we start, we find it virtually impossible to stop. In the fall of 1980, when many of the country's leading sages were declaring the Jimmy Carter–Ronald Reagan contest too close to call, I was lucky enough to call Mr. Reagan in print. In spite of earlier prophecies of mine that had not worked out (I was the very first person to predict that President Muskie would not seek a second term), I became, for some, a semi-prophetic pundit.

If birds gotta fly and fish gotta swim, then predictors have to predict, which accounts, in small part, for the column on Conventional Wisdom which begins this book. It also may help to explain my column of September 23, 1983, in the *Washington Post*, straightforwardly titled "Why Reagan Won't Run," which somewhat diminished my status as a seer.

This has been for me a terrific twelve months. Some of the words and reports in this book obviously did not prove to be timeless, but nothing here has been changed to take advantage of hindsight. If any of this makes you smile, I'll be happy. If any of this allows you to think a little more about politics and a little better about politicians, I'll be happy. But if anything I have written here encourages anyone to get involved in a political campaign, I will be genuinely grateful (especially if it's a Democratic campaign—they really need the help).

Because this book is partly the result of a youth and early middle age spent in the precincts of political America, I first want to thank the men and women of American politics, whose company I have enjoyed and whose skill, dedication and, yes, patriotism I admire.

I am deeply grateful to Meg Greenfield of the *Washington Post*, whose encouragement and friendship helped persuade a political hack that he could learn to type. I especially want to thank Julian Scheer, a good and wise friend, without whose confidence and commitment this book and most of the material in it could not have been produced.

With pressure and under pressure, Kathy Tarut was of invaluable aid in the preparation of this manuscript. Darcy Bacon is an editor and friend whose judgment is only matched by her thoughtfulness.

Finally, I want to thank Anne Hudson Shields and Amy Hudson Shields—my wife and daughter—for their patience and friendship and love.

This book is dedicated to my parents, Mary Fallon Shields and William Francis Shields, who taught their children by word and example that people and politics are both important.

Washington, D.C.　　　　　　　　　　MARK SHIELDS
December, 1984

MARK SHIELDS
On the Campaign Trail

January

Jan. 3 . . . Syria releases captured U.S. flier Lt. Robert Goodman to Rev. Jesse Jackson. Jan. 4 . . . President Reagan welcomes Jackson, Goodman at White House. Jan. 6 . . . First federal matching funds paid to Walter Mondale, John Glenn, Alan Cranston, Reuben Askew, Gary Hart, Ernest Hollings. Jan. 15 . . . Democratic candidates debate in Hanover, New Hampshire. Jan. 22 . . . Raiders win Super Bowl. Jan. 25 . . . Reagan State of the Union Address says "America is back—standing Tall." Jan. 26 . . . Majority of House super delegates endorse Mondale. Jan. 29 . . . Arab funds contributed to Jesse Jackson reported. Jan. 29 . . . Ronald Reagan announces he will run for a second term.

JESSE JACKSON DID THIS...JESSE JACKSON DID THAT...WE'RE SICK OF HEARING ABOUT JESSE JACKSON...

M ost of the nation's conventional political wisdom is produced and consumed right here in Washington. In politics, conventional wisdom (CW) is changed more often than a conscientious driver's motor oil. Recall late October 1979, when Jimmy Carter was already, according to the prevailing CW, a lame duck facing certain defeat at the hands of the charismatic Senator Edward Kennedy. This was prior to Kennedy's interview with Roger Mudd in which the senator qualified for the finals in the Yogi Berra sound-alike contest.

The CW of that time saw Carter's only hope—if he could somehow get by Kennedy—lying in the Republicans' reaffirming their collective death wish by passing over the electable Howard Baker and the acceptable George Bush in favor of the eminently vincible Ronald Reagan. Most wise observers knew that American voters were not about to entrust their fate and future to an ex-Boraxo pitchman. Right!

By February of 1980, the Iranians had taken over our embassy in Teheran, and Jimmy Carter, after becoming the embattled commander in chief, had taken over a big lead in the race for reelection. One reputable national poll showed Carter with a thirty-two-percentage-point lead over both Reagan and Bush. He lost that following November by 8½ million votes to the man he most wanted to run against.

Undaunted and undeterred, the CW salesmen are back. Here are the two hottest current items: 1) Walter Mondale has the 1984 Democratic presidential nomination all locked up, and 2) Ronald Reagan will crush Mondale in November. Once again, beware of conventional wisdom.

The Inevitable Mondale. As Peter Hart, the Mondale pollster, puts it, "The good news is we're way ahead in the polls; the bad news is the polls don't mean much at this stage." One Democratic candidate did polls of the same voters in five states, six weeks apart; the polls showed that 38 percent of the voters changed their choices in those six weeks. This is what analysts call "soft" support, capable of being lost or captured rather easily by an opponent, or even by "undecided."

But with good poll numbers, as Edward Kennedy found out in 1979, come High Expectations. The most recent *Boston Globe* survey of New Hampshire Democrats shows Mondale with the support of nearly half of them and with a three-to-one lead there over Senator John Glenn. What will be "expected" of Fritz Mondale in the candidate debates and the early primaries? Will any perceived slip or slide cost the Minnesotan the loyalty of some of his more pragmatic supporters who had been attracted most by the apparent inevitability of his nomination?

Speaker Thomas P. O'Neill will endorse Mondale in January, and Kennedy is being urged to do likewise by some of his top advisers. Ironically, Mondale could become the victim of his own spectacular success in securing individual and institutional endorsements such as labor, teachers, feminists. With so many bases to touch and feathers not to ruffle on controversial questions, the Mondale campaign will have to fight the temptation to become terminally cautious and the risk of being neutered by saying nothing for fear of offending someone.

Finally, the Democrats are a glandular party that wants to feel. Two months before New Hampshire, Democratic glands remain essentially unstimulated.

The Inevitable Reagan. For the first time in four presidential runs, Ronald Reagan in 1984 should be deprived of his favorite villain—the federal government. He will not be able to campaign against that which he has been running for four years. If 1984 is a referendum on what the voters decided in 1980, then Reagan will be tough to beat. But if the Democrats can frame the election next fall about the future, then Reagan is in large trouble.

Ronald Reagan, president, is beginning to scare people—people who until now had not been scared about or by his presidency. In any foreign involvement, the American people first rally to the president. But extrication is more difficult than involvement, and whatever else Mr. Reagan has done, he has totally failed to mention, let alone inspire, any sense of national sacrifice that would sustain him in rocky times.

After three years of a Reagan presidency, the nation seems closer to war than peace. That could be more important to voters than a three-year tax cut. Beware of conventional wisdom.

* * * * *

The very first event on Ohio Senator John Glenn's New Hampshire campaign schedule was a 6:30 A.M. appearance at the plant gate to greet workers. Long before the sun came up, Senator Glenn stood outside the plant shivering along with a couple of dozen TV and print reporters. The first political rule about factory gates is that the only time for the candidate to meet the workers is when they are coming to work. Then, most workers are willing to postpone the day's labor for a minute or two. But at the end of the day, look out. Even the most popular candidate could get stampeded in the workers' rush to the parking lot and freedom.

What the campaigns want most is a picture on the evening news or in the morning papers. They want their candidate to be seen with American blue-collar workers asking for their votes. Blue-collar workers, as Ronald Reagan understands, are symbolically the contemporary American cowboy, the endangered survivor from an unambiguous era when American males showered after their day's work instead of before. Factory-gate campaigning is intended to show that the candidate is a social democrat (that's with a small "d"), not too self-important to shake the hands and ask for the help of ordinary people who pack a lunch and punch a clock. That's why you can bet every presidential candidate this year, Democrat or Republican, will spend chilly mornings outside factory gates asking for votes and hoping for that picture.

In a match-up with Ronald Reagan, John Glenn, by just about all analyses, comes out with a big advantage. Glenn robs the president of his 1980 themes of patriotism and traditional values. Conceivably Glenn would be able to confront Mr. Reagan on defense by pointing out that, after twenty-three years in the Marine Corps, two wars, and 149 combat missions, he knows a little better than the incumbent where to cut the military fat while protecting and strengthening the muscle.

But that is all in theory and scouting reports. Reality for John Glenn is standing at a plant gate in a state where Walter Mondale, according to everybody's polls, has a commanding lead over Glenn and the rest of the field. John Glenn was friendly to the workers, but the event was a bust. As at every Glenn appearance there were requests for his autograph, but there were no good pictures and Glenn did not introduce himself to, ask the names of, nor ask for the votes of the arriving workers. He was friendly, but diffident.

On paper John Glenn still looks like Ronald Reagan's political nemesis—the small-town boy who became an American hero and success, and who never forgot the people he grew up with. But unless he can catch and defeat Fritz Mondale in New Hampshire, John Glenn will not get the chance to prove what he could do in November.

*   *   *   *   *

When Ronald Reagan was governor of California he had a favorite put-down for the anti-war demonstrators who carried the then-popular sign "Make Love Not War." Of such sign-carrying young men Reagan observed, "The ones I've seen don't look capable of doing either." In 1984, that can't be said of the newest Democratic peace candidate. Jesse Jackson appears quite capable of taking care of himself and anyone else who might care to join the issue in the parking lot.

When Jesse Jackson spoke to a nearly all white pro-environmentalist acid rain conference here in New Hampshire, he exposed many in his audience to an emotional political experience few of them had ever felt before. Jesse Jackson is truly an elemental force. When he speaks of the need for peace there is none of the pacifist divinity student in his voice, no trace of the conciliatory seminarian in his manner. Jesse Jackson communicates strength and he hints at force. There is the unspoken suggestion that those who oppose his brand of peace may run some risks by doing so. He is an

electric presence—probably the most electric political figure
for a live political audience since 1968 when the late Robert
Kennedy and the formidable George Wallace were drawing
huge crowds. I do not know what Jesse Jackson will eventually mean for 1984 or what the year will mean for him, but
because of his exceptional presence this campaign will definitely be changed.

* * * * *

Just about any day now you can expect the first of many
fervent attacks on and indictments of how television has
ruined American politics. Don't you believe it. On balance,
television has made our presidential campaigns more honest
and our candidates more accountable.

No more can a presidential candidate say one thing in
Birmingham, Michigan, and safely say something with just
a little bit different emphasis in Birmingham, Alabama. Of
course, for years the newspapers and wire services have been
reporting what a candidate says, but television can expose
trimming and position-altering by a candidate far more dev-
astatingly than any other medium.

I will also defend television commercials by candidates
where the candidate's message is right there on channel 4 or
44 to be seen by everyone including the opposition. That's
not the way it is, for example, with direct mail, where the
candidate can write to me as a white, Irish, Catholic, middle-
aged homeowner with a family and a mortgage and never
even speak to the families or individuals on either side of me.
Television advertising is more candid. Those are just a couple
of reasons why, when you hear all the castigating and con-
demning of television this year and what it has done to ruin
our politics, you might just want to consider the other side.

* * * * *

Jesse Jackson took a huge political risk. He more than bet
the rent and he more than won. By securing the release of
Navy pilot Lt. Robert Goodman, Jr., from his Syrian captors
and bringing Goodman home, Jesse Jackson single-handedly
changed the politics of 1984.

No longer can Jesse Jackson be described, or dismissed, as simply a gifted phrasemaker; he is now an accomplished peacemaker. How many other candidates in the New Hampshire primary—either Democratic or Republican—can have that said about them?

The immediate political impact will probably be on Jackson's prime constituency—American black voters. Black politicians who have opposed Jackson's candidacy will be hard pressed to argue now that he is not a serious national figure. Black pride in Jackson's achievement will almost inevitably be reflected in increased support for his candidacy among black voters. In the short run, this surge in black support for Jackson will be most bothersome to the Democratic front-runner Walter "Fritz" Mondale, who has been polling well among black voters, in the southern primaries scheduled for March 13 in Alabama, Florida, and Georgia.

But the potential for grave political damage as a result of the Jackson achievement in the Middle East is greatest for Ronald Reagan and the Republicans. Reagan's low standing among black voters was not improved by the fact that before Jackson left for Damascus, he four times refused to accept the Democrat's phone calls. The offered and semi-official explanation for those four refusals—that to do so would have conferred a "legitimacy" upon the trip of a private individual—does not mean much to black Americans who have never felt like the Someone this administration is reaching out to touch.

While Ronald Reagan was not talking to Jesse Jackson, his state department was busy trashing Jackson in the press. Those who believe that diplomacy is the exclusive preserve of people who have tailgated at the Andover-Exeter game were upset by Jackson's mission and unnerved by its success.

* * * * *

As soon as Jackson's accomplishment in bringing back Lt. Goodman became clear, Ronald Reagan publicly conceded.

At the White House welcoming ceremony, the president graciously accepted his supporting role. One reason Ronald Reagan is personally liked by a majority of the electorate is that he handles the public, ceremonial duties of his office so well.

One only has to imagine how other recent chief executives might have handled the White House welcome for freed Navy pilot Lt. Robert Goodman and his liberator.

President Jimmy Carter. First, for twenty minutes, President Carter painstakingly explained the legislative history of the Logan Act, which forbids private citizens from conducting American foreign policy. He then reminded his audience that Syrian President Hafez Assad had been Mr. Carter's "very close, personal friend," long before Rev. Jackson had met him. For the first time, Mr. Carter publicly revealed that he had experienced difficulty in sleeping since Lt. Goodman's capture and that, as a result, he had been working an average of 19½ hours every day.

President Gerald Ford. Warm laughter filled the White House room and eased the tension when President Ford welcomed his two visitors as "Lt. Jackson and Rev. Goodman." Becoming aware of the mix-up, the president then smiled broadly, corrected himself, and saluted Jackson for "demonstrating conclusively that the private sector, free of governmental interference, is unstoppable."

President Richard Nixon. President Nixon observed that his welcoming of Jesse Jackson and Lt. Goodman constituted "an authentic, historic first for this president and the presidency." Mr. Nixon, who had reportedly been furious at the Jackson trip and displeased with the Syrians, said that any "public division" over Administration Mideast policy was "entirely fabricated" by "narrow partisans who prefer the easy course" in collaboration with publishers who "refuse to accept the 1972 election results." Mr. Nixon was joined by entertainer Sammy Davis, Jr., who, he said, would go with him and Jackson and Goodman to a professional basketball game that night. Mr. Nixon then gave a surprised Lt. Goodman what the White House press office later described as a Whittier College version of the High Five.

Every president is compared to his predecessors, something for which Mr. Reagan ought to be grateful.

The Super Bowl game next Sunday recalls an established political rule. Every politician would rather have his name or picture on the sports page than on the front page. Most politicians will do nearly anything to identify with sports and especially with a winning hometown team.

The values of sports are ones with which most Americans can easily identify. Sports are relentlessly democratic. When someone is trying to hit a curve ball or catch a forward pass, it makes no difference whether his ancestors arrived at Plymouth on the *Mayflower* or within the last calendar year with English as a second language. For many American newcomers, sports have been a way up and a way out. So politicians understandably welcome every chance to be seen in the company of popular athletes.

For those Americans who are genuine sports fans, cheering at the ball park for their favorite team is a release, a chance to get away from bills, work, and worry—which frequently includes elected politicians. So when any politician is too obvious in his self-promotion at a sports event, he runs the risk of being loudly and publicly booed. I've seen it happen.

Because he is both a politician and a sports fan, President Reagan will almost surely telephone the winner's locker room after the Super Bowl. Let's just hope this one doesn't last as long as the president's last locker-room call to the Baltimore Orioles after they won the 1983 World Series. That's when everyone from the groundskeeper to the batboy seemed to get on the phone. But you can't blame him; sports are more popular than politics. That's why politicians have been trying to go steady with sports for a long time.

* * * * *

Council Bluffs, Iowa — If his 1984 campaign is a reliable guide to the personality and character of Walter ("Fritz") Mondale—and there is no reason to believe that it would not be—then Mondale, if elected, would be the most thorough, as little-to-chance-leaving president in recorded history.

The evidence for this conclusion was gathered in a recent two-day swing through Iowa with the Democratic front runner. First, please understand that, regardless of our righteous

railing against candidates' catering to special-interest constituencies, we in the political press constitute an identifiable
group with specific interests of our own. Those interests,
which the Mondale campaign anticipates and attends to,
include the predictability of the candidate's public schedule
and the availability of press facilities such as phones. An established political maxim holds that any presidential candidate who cannot effectively organize a presidential campaign
shows himself incapable of being president. That seems fair.
But through its relentless efficiency the Mondale campaign
may be converting some observers to that maxim's corollary:
the candidate who can organize a top-flight presidential campaign could probably also run the United States government.

Of course, every campaign succeeds or fails ultimately on
the strengths and skills of the candidate. But a rested, un-
hassled press corps may be marginally less captious and
critical. When the press is told accurately that the traveling
party will arrive in Central City at eight P.M., then the press
can make plans to see an old flame or a new movie at eight-
thirty, which puts the press in a better mood and may put
the candidate in the way of better press.

*   *   *   *   *

In New Hampshire there is one underdog candidate who
deserves our help and encouragement. This underdog has no
headquarters, no pricey media consultant, no canny press
secretary. Our candidate doesn't even have a first name;
maybe that's the reason every other important candidate feels
free to pick on him.

The name of our candidate is "Expected." You remember
the last Iowa caucus, the last primary in New Hampshire?
What did every losing candidate give as excuse and explanation for his lousy showing? The same thing they'll undoubtedly say this time: "We did better than expected." Even the
candidates who finished dead last said it. It's no wonder they
did better than Expected, because Expected never had a
volunteer, a bumper sticker, or a button. Did you ever see
Expected on the Phil Donahue Show or perched on Merv
Griffin's couch? Of course not. Well, the traditional American

spirit of fair play will not be denied. Let's all urge voters to write in the name of Expected, so that Expected will no longer be the lowest standard of political performance which all candidates can say they did better than. Let's make this the year that Expected actually does better than anticipated. Next time we can help Anticipated.

February

Feb. 1 . . . *Tip O'Neill endorses Walter Mondale.* **Feb. 7** *. . . Reagan orders Marines out of Lebanon.* **Feb. 9** *. . . Soviet President Andropov dies; Chernenko selected.* **Feb. 11** *. . . Democrats debate in Iowa.* **Feb. 20** *. . . Mondale wins Iowa Democratic caucuses by wide margin; Glenn finishes 5th. Gary Hart finishes ahead of the rest of the candidates, in 2nd place. John Glenn overhauls his campaign staff. Ronald Reagan campaigns in Iowa.* **Feb. 26** *. . . Jesse Jackson apologizes in New Hampshire for referring to Jews as Hymies.* **Feb. 28** *. . . Hart upsets Mondale in New Hampshire primary.* **Feb. 29** *. . . Cranston withdraws from race.*

"HERE'S A NUMBER FOR YOU... 87% OF THE PEOPLE HATE POPULARITY POLLS!"

An established political rule was on display in Washington again last week, when major personnel changes and staff shake-ups were announced in Senator John Glenn's presidential campaign. The rule: "It's a lot easier and safer for critics to criticize the staff of a powerful and popular politician than to criticize directly the popular and powerful politician."

Several dozen drumbeats of criticism preceded the leadership changes in the Glenn presidential campaign. Most of the criticism was directed toward the senator's long-time friend and aide, Bill White, who was basically kicked upstairs in the shake-up. That's generally the pattern here in Washington.

Long before President Richard Nixon was roundly roasted for the sins of his campaign and administration, we in the press were boldly criticizing his top lieutenants, Haldeman and Erlichman.

Later, before Jimmy Carter was personally faulted for failing to provide consistent leadership, there was widespread criticism of the Georgians in his White House. The fact is that criticizing the staff of a powerful politician is a cop-out. Nobody inherits a staff. The staff is picked and retained by the man at the top, and every campaign inevitably reflects the person who is the candidate. The fault, if there is any, is not with the staff but with the candidate, in this case with John Glenn.

* * * * *

Ronald Reagan has one large, frequently overlooked advantage as he seeks a second four-year term in the White House. He will be the first president since Dwight Eisenhower some twenty-eight years ago not to be challenged for renomination within his own party.

Ronald Reagan owns the heart, the mind, and, yes, the glands of the Republican party. This fact is universally conceded within the GOP, the result being that no registered Republican holding elected office above that of assistant library board trustee will challenge the president's renomination. This is for Ronald Reagan a genuine advantage in seek-

ing to become the first president since Richard Nixon to win
reelection. In 1968, President Lyndon Johnson, facing challenges from Senator Gene McCarthy and Senator Robert
Kennedy, chose not to run and obviously was not reelected.
In 1976, President Jerry Ford was challenged by Ronald
Reagan (that was the year Mr. Reagan wanted to put exact
change lanes in the Panama Canal) and Ford lost in November to Jimmy Carter who, four years later, beat back a
primary challenge by Ted Kennedy and was beaten in November. Primary challenges do not spontaneously arise; they
occur when a president is already vulnerable. And even when
repulsed, they strip the advantage of incumbency. With no
primary challenge to him, Ronald Reagan will be free to be
"presidential" during the spring and summer of 1984.

* * * * *

The White House has announced that President Reagan,
now an announced candidate for reelection, will visit what
Ronald Reagan used to call "Red China." In 1972, President
Nixon, a longtime foe of the Peking regime and, like Mr.
Reagan, a defender of Chiang Kai-shek and the Nationalist
Chinese forces on Taiwan, visited the People's Republic in a
historic first. In 1976, Mr. Nixon visited China again just before that year's New Hampshire primary where Gerald Ford
was being challenged by Mr. Reagan who was then criticizing the Ford-Kissinger soft line on foreign policy. For some
reason during election years conservative anti-communist
presidents have concluded that it's good luck to have their
pictures taken in the company of short communists.

* * * * *

National defense and America's role in the world will almost certainly be central to the national debate in the presidential campaign of 1984. And at the heart of that debate will
be the question of who serves and who doesn't in defending
the United States and whose lives could be risked and
perhaps lost.

Only one presidential candidate, South Carolina Democratic Senator Ernest ("Fritz"), Hollings, has come out cate-

gorically in favor of the restoration of the military draft. Hollings objects to letting the burden of defending the nation fall exclusively upon the sons of America's working class and low-income families, especially blacks and Hispanics. All the other candidates, including the president, more or less support the present volunteer army. The administration, in support of the volunteer army, points out that the percentage of new recruits who are high school graduates jumped from 68 percent in 1980 to 81 percent in 1981. That is encouraging, but it happened at a time when hiring was down and layoffs were up in this country, and it was followed by the highest unemployment rate since Pearl Harbor. The true question will be confronted if the Kemp-Roth/Reagan plan works and produces those promised thirteen million new jobs. Then high school graduates will have a choice of civilian opportunities and the nation will find out whether we in the United States can defend ourselves without bothering the privileged classes.

* * * * *

Presidential candidates almost always welcome and appreciate endorsements of their candidacy by prominent and popular politicians. But sometimes the delay in those endorsements makes them less welcome and less appreciated than they would have been earlier.

Late last September the Democratic presidential race looked a lot more competitive than it does right now. The big event on the schedule for Saturday, October 1, was a straw vote among the delegates to the Maine Democratic convention. For then-frontrunner Walter Mondale the Maine straw vote became semicrucial. He had earlier been upset in Wisconsin by Senator Alan Cranston and needed a comeback victory to show that Wisconsin had been only an aberration. Maine has a Democratic governor, Joe Brennan, and a Democratic senator, George Mitchell. Both men spurned all requests to endorse Mondale before that straw vote. Mondale won in Maine without the endorsements.

This past weekend, four months later, Governor Brennan

and Senator Mitchell both endorsed Mondale. Nobody could really blame Fritz Mondale if he recalled John Kennedy's line about the governor at the 1960 convention who said he would support Kennedy not on the critical first ballot but on a hypothetical second ballot: "As he's with me more and more, I need him less and less."

Postscript: Less than one month later, both Senator Mitchell and Governor Brennan proved that their endorsements were not lightly given. Five days after his upset defeat in the New Hampshire primary, Mondale faced the Maine delegate caucuses. Although Mondale lost in Maine, both Brennan and Mitchell, in the parlance of politics, went to the mattresses for their candidate.

* * * * *

Massachusetts — This is the time in a presidential campaign when the dark-horse candidates, sensing that time is no longer their ally, are likely to take a chance—to make a bold or controversial statement in hopes of getting the voters' attention and maybe their approval, too.

Nobody knows better than presidential candidates the immutable laws of primary politics, and the first is that no one has been elected president since Harry Truman without first winning the New Hampshire primary. Nobody can survive in presidential primaries with a string of second- or third-place finishes. Chrysler's Lee Iacocca is toasted as a genius for bringing his company up to a "solid third." In politics there's no such thing. So now successful politicians like Senator Gary Hart of Colorado and Senator Alan Cranston of California can see their long-shot campaigns facing that moment of truth. Their message is delivered with greater urgency.

In Iowa the other day Gary Hart criticized the front runner, former Vice-President Fritz Mondale, for privately opposing as vice-president unpopular decisions on the grain embargo, draft registration, the MX missile, and the sale of arms to Saudi Arabia. Hart posed a question: "Was there ever an issue where President Carter took a popular position and Vice-President Mondale opposed him in private, or did Mr. Mondale dissent only from decisions that now appear to be politically unpopular?" It's that time in a campaign when chances are taken, when the gloves come off, and when real damage can be inflicted.

* * * * *

Recent disclosures about the Arab League contributing $200,000 to civil rights organizations closely identified with Jesse Jackson, and attacks upon Jackson by Jewish spokesmen as well as verbal retaliation by Jackson supporters, have the Republicans happily anticipating a political civil war between the Democratic party's two most loyal constituencies, black voters and Jewish voters.

A number of Jewish voters have had misgivings about Jesse Jackson since 1979 when Jackson's chummy visit with PLO leader Yasser Arafat was captured and preserved in photographs. Last week the national director of the Anti-Defamation League said the Arab League was "evidently making an investment in someone they have confidence in." Jackson supporters responded by pointing out that in 1982 Jewish political action committees contributed $1.7 million to congressional candidates. The emotional thermostat has been turned up. Jackson has called for the creation of a Palestinian homeland in the Middle East. This issue has been avoided by the Democratic party's leadership since the 1967 Arab-Israeli war. It's the kind of human rights question that could produce a genuine brawl at next July's San Francisco convention and force the Democratic nominee to choose between the all-out support of Jesse Jackson and a lot of American Jewish voters. Right now, Jewish-black tension means political trouble for the Democrats and opportunity for the Republicans.

* * * * *

Massachusetts — One traditional way of measuring political support is to count the candidates' bumper stickers on various cars and vehicles. I just took a poll here in Massachusetts on bumper stickers, and the results may surprise you as much as they did me.

With both the New Hampshire and Massachusetts presidential primaries taking place within the next four weeks, the campaigning here has been intense. But all the presidential candidates together are trailing radio stations by a margin of four to one. I don't know what future anthropologists will tell us it meant that Americans in 1984 identified more passionately and publicly with radio stations that promised "More rock—less talk" or "Country Cool" than with presidential candidates who pledged a nuclear freeze or a balanced budget.

*   *   *   *   *

The bickering among Democratic presidential candidates Walter Mondale, John Glenn, and Gary Hart over the role and influence of organized labor in the Democrats' nomination fight brims with hypocrisy but it also reflects and reveals a fundamental truth about the Democratic party in 1984.

In their first nine years in the Senate, Hart and Glenn have voted right—according to the AFL-CIO definition of what's right—eight out of every ten times on issues of importance to that labor group. In their successful campaigns, Hart and Glenn both welcomed the endorsement of the AFL-CIO. But now, to Hart's and Glenn's disappointment, the AFL-CIO has endorsed Walter Mondale for president. In his twelve years in the Senate, Mondale voted with labor nine out of every ten times. What is interesting is the fact that Glenn and Hart challenged Mondale to identify only where he disagrees with labor. Organized labor is The Heavy from which candidates are expected to distance themselves. Labor is not fashionable. Mondale is not publicly cross-examined by his opponents on where he disagrees with environmentalists, feminists, or gays. Maybe those groups are considered too noble to have stooges. For whatever reasons, the Democrats are careful not to criticize them. Labor, which is easy to caricature, is available for cheap shots. It is not gifted at public relations and, as a result, one of the few institutions less popular than Labor is Big Labor. But nobody ever won an election running against tiny defense contractors or medium-sized government, either.

*   *   *   *   *

In Iowa on Monday night there were eight Democratic presidential candidates. There was a contest. One candidate, the front runner and former vice-president in the Carter administration, Walter Mondale, won. Everybody else, including Senator Gary Hart of Colorado and former Senator George McGovern, did not win. Most especially Senator John Glenn did not win. Viewers and voters may have been confused on Monday night and Tuesday morning when they heard various network anchor people congratulate Senator Hart on finishing a strong second with 15 percent of the vote. That means he did not get 85 percent of the vote. NBC called Hart's showing impressive and the Iowa results a very big victory for Gary Hart. Maybe somebody should get in touch with President Gerald Ford, who won 49 percent of the national vote in 1976. All Jerry Ford got was an eviction notice from his government housing and the title of ex-president. Remember, winning is coming in first.

The author's "winning is coming in first" rule was amended following this year's Iowa caucus and subsequent New Hampshire primary results. But, in the interest of full disclosure this dispatch is included. Who knows, it may prove to be right some other year.

* * * * *

Running for president is strictly a voluntary activity on the part of those who do so. In all cases, it is also the bold act of a strong ego. Few captains of industry, academe, or journalism would be willing to expose their egos or themselves to the scrutiny, the indifference, and the heartbreak of a presidential campaign where everyone the candidate ever double-dated with knows the morning after the New Hampshire primary whether their old friend is among the many who lose or the few who win.

Take a couple of this year's darkest horses who, if the polls are correct, will not be making an acceptance speech at the Democratic convention next July in San Francisco. As Florida governor, Reuben Askew enacted that state's first corporate income tax, appointed the South's first black supreme court judge, and wrote an environmental plan which stood as a model for the nation. As governor of and senator from South Carolina, Fritz Hollings changed the direction of his party and the destiny of his state, and, as much as any American, he was responsible for the repeal of the oil depletion allowance loophole that had made tax avoidance legal for generations of rich Texans. Yet, if neither man becomes the nominee of his party, both will be remembered, and referred to by many, merely as unsuccessful presidential candidates. How many people remember George Romney as the able Republican governor of Michigan rather than as the presidential candidate who confessed to having been "brainwashed" about Vietnam? It's a tough business and it can be cruel.

* * * * *

This is a hypothetical. Imagine, if you would, that a newspaper of the stature and circulation of the *Washington Post* had reported in a front-page story that Edwin Meese, III, the attorney general-designate, referred, in private conversation with reporters, to American Jews as "Hymies" and to New York City as "Hymietown." How many senators—Democrats and Republicans—would have been injured in the stampede to the Senate press gallery where Meese's withdrawal/resignation would have been unanimously demanded? How many gentlemen and gentlewomen of the cloth would have called publicly for the sacking of Meese? How many columnists would have exhausted our annual ration of indignation denouncing Meese's shameful behavior? The answer, you can be sure, would have been a number larger than the combined totals of the first five finishers in the Iowa presidential caucuses.

For uttering ethnic or racial references far less offensive than those allegedly made by candidate Jackson, other politicians have been hounded by camera crews and microphones and harangued by their political opponents. Who can forget Spiro Agnew calling a reporter on his campaign plane a "fat Jap," considered conclusive evidence of Agnew's moral cretinism?

Would Democratic candidates Mondale, McGovern, Hollings, Hart, Glenn, Askew, and Cranston have been so silent if the same *Post* story had been published about Ed Meese?

Even more important than what Jackson does or doesn't say by way of explanation is the deafening silence on the part of most of the press and political world. These same folks rightly called Nixon's taped transcripts "shabby" and "disgraceful" and Earl Butz worse. Why the apparent double standard for a presidential candidate who happens to be black? Why the lack of curiosity and cross-examination? Do we expect less of a black presidential candidate than of Spiro Agnew or Earl Butz?

❖　❖　❖　❖　❖

Up to now the 1984 Democratic campaign has had a front runner but lacked its own distinctive dialogue. Those conditions may have been reversed by Gary Hart's dramatic victory in New Hampshire. If the Coloradan is successful in determining the language of the Democratic debate in the next two weeks, the fight will be between the New and Future (Hart) against the Old and Past (Mondale). If Mondale does win the nomination, after being tagged as the candidate of the past, his general-election mission will be made that much more difficult.

After New Hampshire, Mondale is no longer the undisputed nominee-to-be with the best chance to beat Reagan, which had been the strongest argument made by black politicians for endorsing him. Minority voters—like Catholics in 1960 and Southerners in 1976—tend to ignore differences and disagreements with the first candidate from their group to be considered for an important office. Bruised by the controversy over his use of anti-Jewish terms, and by the need to apologize, Jesse Jackson will find electoral solace in Dixie.

❖　❖　❖　❖　❖

To understand the jargon and the slang of American politics, something that has to be especially difficult for the many non-English-speaking journalists who are assigned to our presidential campaign, it is important to be familiar with bakeries.

If you think about it, politics has appropriated for its own use the metaphor of the bakery. For example, a vigorous economy, which is favored by all candidates, is referred to as a growing economic pie. But even a growing economic pie does not preclude some hard choices. Because, as we have learned by now, you can't have your cake and eat it too. The candidate who talks about the real problems of people—like what we pay for rent, heat, food, and education—is dealing with bread-and-butter issues, no matter how you slice it. And what do we say about someone like Colorado Senator Gary Hart, whose face will almost surely be on next week's covers of *Newsweek* and *Time* and for whom things seem to be going quite well right now? Of course, we use another bakery expression. This week Gary Hart is on a roll.

March

Mar. 1 . . . *Glenn describes himself as "the new underdog." Hollings, Askew take themselves out of contention.* Mar. 4 . . . *Hart criticizes Mondale at Boston dinner. Hart wins Maine caucuses.* Mar. 6 . . . *Hart wins Vermont preference vote.* Mar. 8 . . . *Gallup poll shows Hart leading Reagan 52%-43%.* Mar. 11 . . . *Mondale asks "Where's the Beef?" in the Atlanta debate.* Mar. 13 . . . *Super Tuesday—Hart wins Massachusetts, Rhode Island, Florida; Mondale wins Alabama and Georgia.* Mar. 14 . . . *McGovern withdraws from race.* Mar. 16 . . . *Glenn withdraws from the race.* Mar. 20 . . . *Mondale beats Hart in Illinois.* Mar. 27 . . . *Hart wins Connecticut primary.* Mar. 28 . . . *New York debate moderated by Dan Rather.*

Senator John Glenn, who had been expected to be one of the main two contenders for the Democratic presidential nomination, has managed to collect only 13 percent of the total vote in Iowa and New Hampshire. Glenn has lost a couple of political contests, but he has not lost either his sense of balance or his sense of humor.

On the night of Iowa, where he won just 3.5 percent of the caucus vote, John Glenn was cheering up his campaign workers and volunteers, telling them, "I don't want to see any sad faces." All week long Glenn has been "up," even though he had to know the Iowa results had given him as much of a letdown as they've given Gary Hart a lift. Glenn was classy on his way to a bad third-place finish. In the New Hampshire debate he kidded himself by saying, "I may be dull, but I'm not boring." At his election day press conference Glenn was asked by a journalist about the $2.5 million loan his campaign had received from several Ohio banks. To the question about the bank transaction—What did Glenn do with the 650 toasters the bank would have given him?—John Glenn laughed heartily and insisted that all the toasters were 100 percent American made, which should please organized labor. For those who saw him this week in New Hampshire, John Glenn had the right stuff. He just didn't have the votes.

* * * * *

TO: Walter F. Mondale
FROM: Mark Shields, *Washington Post*, March 1984
Sir: Sorry about New Hampshire. Cannot overemphasize now that time is not your ally. Incredible as it may seem after all you've accomplished over the last two years, this nomination can get away from you by the end of this month. This weekend you are still on the slippery slope. Urgent action is required.

The heart of the matter is this: Americans, which includes Democrats, are mostly incurable optimists. They equate change with improvement. For fifty years Democrats generally represented change in the nation's politics. In 1980

Ronald Reagan took that away; he seized the change side of the national political equation. Against Reagan, the Democrats became the party of the status quo—and suffered a devastating defeat.

In New Hampshire, Senator Gary Hart seized the change side of the equation in this year's Democratic presidential politics.

Consider the last few weeks. On the day of the Iowa caucuses you led Hart in New Hampshire 41 percent to 10 percent. Eight days later he beat you 41 percent to 29 percent. Now television has told the whole country that Hart is the candidate of "the future" and "new ideas," while some of your supporters have demonstrated the eloquence of an OSHA regulation for water closets; this is no time to be talking about who has the most delegate slates in Pennsylvania, or who knows the winner-take-all loopholes in Casper, Wyoming.

Luckily it won't matter much what your spokespeople are saying. In politics, only the candidate—you—can give a campaign clear definition and meaning for the voters. You have failed to do this so far, but you simply must do it before March 20. You must take personal responsibility for defining your campaign. Your talented advisers and consultants can only refine a message; you must define it.

Ask yourself these questions: What will you tell your grandchildren in 2004 when they ask, "Grandpa, why did you run for president in 1984?" If you could only accomplish two things in your first term as president, what would they be? I'm not looking here for an omnibus Safe Streets and Happy Ever After Act, but for tangible goals that people can identify with—and identify you with.

Up to now, your agenda has sounded too much like the 1980 Democratic platform, the one that solemnly promised "federally funded teacher centers in every state to address such issues as bilingual, multicultural-non-racist, and non-sexist curricula." (Honest—page 39.) You simply cannot run on a program of restoring Reagan's budget cuts, formal validation of bizarre personal behavior, general abdication of any and all American responsibilities overseas—and repeal of the third year of the Reagan tax cut.

Here are some recommendations for how to proceed:

* Try to be a little less Norwegian. The vote for president is the most personal vote any American casts. To vote for you, they have to feel they know you personally, and like you. You must be ready to risk revealing more of your private self in this campaign—yourself, and your sense of humor.

* Don't be afraid to be funny. For most people you are still a walking resume of the jobs you've held, not a person with feelings and family. You could kid about the vice-presidency, which a lot of people are predisposed to believe is kind of funny. You might tell audiences that being VP is such an anonymous job that when you had it, a Gallup Poll found that 74 percent of the public thought "Mondale" was a suburb of Los Angeles.

* Establish your independence in a hurry. "Overpromising" is a real problem; so is your close identification with unions and other interest groups. Voters rightly want proof that a presidential candidate isn't a prisoner of his past—that he hasn't subcontracted out his independence. Your supporters have to realize this too; they can't get much out of you if you don't win this thing. There's little they can do if you now advertise your independence from them—and they ought to realize that this would be smart for all of you. Voters must see you telling some semi-powerful group what they don't want to hear.

* Stick to your anti-Establishment position on trade. You have already taken near-unanimous criticism for your pro-American position on our trading partners' unfair practices. This is a genuinely populist issue where Reagan and Senator Hart line up with the Establishment and you have only the people on your side.

* From now on, worry more about your media message than about your organization.

Organization is important, especially in caucus states like

Maine today, and especially at the beginning of the political season. But now, after just two weeks, television has taken over. Nobody can organize separate campaigns on the same day in Florida, Massachusetts, Alabama, and Georgia. No longer does a surfeit of candidates dilute the coverage. The networks have what they like best—a head-to-head contest of at most three contestants. The people you need to reach now are not going to respond to a canvass. They're going to respond to you—the Fritz Mondale they'll see on television.

Gary Hart has stolen the spotlight, but the media are still giving you equal attention; they need you if only to keep their horse race alive.

* Stay calm during the inevitable rough going-over from the news media. Within a week you will know how John Glenn has felt for the past six months. Only a week ago your "loyal" careerists were picking out their White House parking spaces; now they're explaining, on background, where your campaign went wrong. A political operation that was previously praised as a model of technical perfection will now be damned as the Imperial Candidacy. Your success in winning endorsements from an incredible range of Democratic leaders will now be written off as Muskie Revisited.

The manner in which you take this inevitable criticism will be important. Don't be testy or defensive. Voters respect leaders who can take their knocks with equanimity.

* Don't be afraid to challenge your fellow citizens—you can let Reagan have the selfishness issue.

Americans respond to calls for collective action. They believe in sacrifice for a common good. They believe in national—as opposed to personal—interest.

Let Reagan ask them, Are you better off than you were four years ago? Mondale should ask if *we* are better off after four years of Reagan—are we stronger as a society, better off as a people?

This year Ronald Reagan and the Republicans will be trying mightily to rerun the election of 1980, and you can't really blame them. After all, the Democrats ran against

Herbert Hoover for forty years; the Republicans can run against Jimmy Carter at least twice.

Democrats don't like to think much about what happened in 1980. When they won back twenty-six House seats in 1982 merely by exploiting the misery created by Reagan's recession, they completely lost sight of the lessons of '80. But those lessons must be learned if any Democrat is to win the White House.

Tell voters where you want to lead our nation: Give them your vision for the future—a vision larger than any legislative program and based on values. Articulate our national interest and what we must all do to protect it and make the world a safer place. Patriotism means more than just paying higher taxes. Summon the best in all of us to make a more just American family.

* * * * *

What is the first question we ask of anyone who personally knows someone who is famous? Usually it is, "What is he or she really like?" Is this person mean, or decent, or thoughtful, or rude? In politics that is called the character question. And those are the questions now being asked about Senator Gary Hart, who is sweeping through the political world like either a tidal wave or a prairie fire or both.

Everywhere you turn someone is reporting on Gary Hart. We have learned that he is a loner, born in Kansas, not a back-slapper or a hail-fellow-well-met. That he works hard in the Senate, studies issues diligently. Those are the recurring points that have been made, but now people are looking at Gary Hart differently than they did only eight days ago. Now they search for telltale signs of character. Sunday night in Boston, at a Democratic dinner where it had just been announced that Gary Hart was winning in Maine over Walter Mondale, Hart broke a rule. He said that Mondale would not claim the title of front runner again, and that he would "rather be considered a little-known dark horse struggling to get by on twelve million dollars and an AFL-CIO endorsement." Eight days earlier, when Gary Hart was a genuine underdog, such a verbal jab was perfectly okay. But now he is a winner. And in the tribal rules of politics, winners are supposed to be generous and gracious. In Boston, Gary Hart was neither. It is all part of answering the question, "What kind of a guy is he?"

* * * * *

The casualty list left in the wake of the popular explosion of Colorado Senator Gary Hart in the Democratic presidential race continues to grow. In addition to a handful of vanquished candidacies and a bushel of bruised journalistic egos, the victims include several pet theories about which much less will be heard later. Here is a short list of pet theories curbed by the Hart upset victories—each of which the candidate, with characteristic modesty, calls a "miracle."

The Polls Pick the Winner. On February 12, just two weeks before the New Hampshire primary, the Gallup poll found that former Vice-President Walter Mondale was the presidential choice of 49 percent of the Democrats. In distant second were Jesse Jackson with 14 percent and Senator John Glenn with 13 percent. Next came George McGovern and Reuben Askew, each with 3 percent of the votes. Tied with Fritz Hollings and Alan Cranston at 2 percent (down from a lofty 5 percent the previous fall) was a fellow who appeared to be running to prepare himself for a serious 1988 race: Gary Hart of Colorado.

Now Hart is proving that polls reflect rather than dictate public opinion.

You Can't Beat Money in Presidential Politics. As of February 1, the Hart campaign had raised a little over $2.2 million and was $555,000 in debt. By comparison, Mondale had raised $14.4 million and still had an on-hand war chest of over $2 million. Glenn, Cranston, and Askew had all raised more money than Hart.

Like the polls, political money frequently follows public support. Since the New Hampshire upset, hitherto unnoticed virtues of character and intellect in Gary Hart have been discovered by political contributors who had prematurely sighted similar qualities in Walter Mondale and John Glenn. After next Tuesday, the Hart fundraising people will probably be so inundated with contributors' calls that the campaign could use an unlisted number.

Before the Primaries Begin "They" Have Already Picked the Winner. This year's "they" included organized labor, teachers unions, feminist and environmentalist groups, leading elected and unelected politicians, and most of the political press—which concluded that Mondale either should or was certain to be the Democratic presidential nominee in 1984.

The unfolding scenario was clear to the semi-astute observer: The "Democrats" had privately agreed that Mondale would be the candidate. Overlooked was the fact that endorsements mean more on checks than for presidential candidates, and that in national politics, nobody—but nobody—delivers anybody else's vote.

* * * * *

Most successful office-seekers are endowed with an extra olfactory gland that enables its owner to sniff political winds before the rest of us can. That helps explain why, in the two weeks immediately following the New Hampshire loss, the Mondale campaign was forced to learn what it was like to be put—rather than to put others—on Hold. Politicians who only days earlier had been elbowing their way onto public platforms to be seen with the former vice-president could not be found. They suddenly remembered an unbreakable appointment with the family taxidermist or a command performance at a nephew's graduation from driving school. This disappearing act is known as "doing a Dixie" or "going South" on someone. At the top of the short and distinguished list of politicians who did not do a Dixie on Fritz Mondale, after New Hampshire, is Massachusetts Governor Michael Dukakis.

Defeat can be a most reliable antidote for arrogance. Before New Hampshire, arrogance had been no stranger to the Mondale campaign. Prior to his own stunning upset defeat in his state's 1978 gubernatorial primary, self-doubt and Michael Dukakis had never spent much time together.

For whatever reason, the Mondale defeat in New Hampshire appeared to energize Dukakis, who realized early on that Senator Gary Hart and the Massachusetts Democrats were a matched pair. Dukakis campaigned across the state from New Bedford to Springfield, appearing at plant gates, on television, and in parades in behalf of Mondale. He persuaded some of his most gifted people to help Mondale full time and he left no doubt in anyone's mind what his endorsement meant.

While being able to smell a winner says something about a politician's intuition, sticking with a candidate he's endorsed—in the face of certain defeat—says a lot more about that politician's integrity.

* * * * *

Do you remember a couple of years back when it looked for sure like the 1984 Democratic presidential struggle would be between Senator Ted Kennedy and former Vice-President Fritz Mondale? At that time, some Mondale loyalists were not too eager to run against a Kennedy. As one said at the time, it's always a problem running against a legend or a myth. Then Senator Kennedy announced he would not run in 1984, thus ending Mondale's worries in that direction. Well, not exactly.

A political reporter traveling in the primary states is struck by voters' responses to the question: Why are they supporting Gary Hart about whom they admit they know very little? One of the reasons obviously is that many of the Democratic voters have problems with Mr. Mondale; his closeness to big labor is frequently cited. Some Hart supporters mention the Colorado senator's new ideas. But a lot more mention the fact that he reminds them of President John Kennedy and of a time when Americans were united in pride for their country, when most Americans were confident we could do just about anything we set our minds and wills to do. A lot has happened since then to dampen national optimism. But Americans still yearn for that happier time, and Fritz Mondale, who thought when Massachusetts's senior senator pulled

out of the 1984 race that he would not be competing with any of the Kennedy magic or myth, finds himself being compared to a Kennedy named Hart.

*   *   *   *   *

In the two weeks after New Hampshire and before Super Tuesday, Mondale was able to make the case—at least for some voters—why Gary Hart should not be their first choice for president. What Mondale has been unable to make, except to the demographic base of the Democratic party, is the case for why he should be president.

The two surviving Democratic challengers reminded one party activist, this week, of Disraeli's qualifications for political leadership—that a man know himself and that he also know his times. In the middle of March of 1984, the questions are whether Fritz Mondale, who seems to know himself quite well, understands today's times and tomorrow; and whether Gary Hart, who seems remarkably in tune with the times, knows himself. The answers will in large measure determine who is the Democratic nominee and whether the nation gets a new president next January.

* * * * *

1984 has not been a very good year for predictions or for the people who make them. By now Fritz Mondale was supposed to have wrapped up the Democratic nomination unless, of course, Senator John Glenn stopped him. Here is a sure-fire, lead-pipe cinch prediction about the Democratic convention in San Francisco next July.

Do you remember the 1980 convention? There were two semi-memorable speeches that year: Ronald Reagan's acceptance speech in Detroit, and Ted Kennedy's non-acceptance speech in Madison Square Garden. Let me go on record right now. At next July's Democratic convention, regardless of who is nominated, the most talked about and guaranteed-to-be-remembered speech will be made by Jesse Jackson. Sometimes on the evening news—like Kennedy in 1980—Jesse Jackson seems to be yelling, to be a trifle too hot for the conversational medium which is television. But at a convention in a huge hall with thousands of people listening and cheering, television viewers understand that a speaker must nearly shout. Jesse Jackson is in for the long haul and at the San Francisco convention he will give a speech that will be compared to William Jennings Bryan's "Cross of Gold" speech. It's one prediction you can count on.

* * * * *

There, on this week's "Tuesday Night at the Fights," was Kid Comeback (a.k.a. Minnesota Fritz) accepting congratulations for his big Illinois win. Four weeks ago, before New Hampshire, he had been extremely confident and above the fray. Last week, after turning feisty scrapper, he had been saved by the bell in Dixie. The experience, he told voters, had made him a changed man, a better candidate who would be a better president. On Tuesday night, the networks asked

him to define the differences between the Colorado contender
and himself. Kid Comeback did not flinch. He immediately
confronted one of the truly critical issues of our time: he is
totally committed to moving the United States embassy in
Israel from Tel Aviv to Jerusalem while his opponent is late
or otherwise unreliable on the matter of the embassy move.

Mondale told his television listeners three things when he
chose that difference. First, that he knows the next big primary is New York where up to one-third of the Democratic
electorate is Jewish. Second, that he apparently believes
American Jewish voters can be wooed and won on the
embassy-transfer issue. And third, that Fritz Mondale has
not really changed very much since New Hampshire, where
voters were turned off by his overly cozy relationships
with organized labor, teachers' unions, and other prominent
endorsers.

* * * * *

In a funny way the 1984 Democratic presidential race is
beginning to resemble strongly the 1980 fall presidential campaign. And the part of Jimmy Carter is being played this time
by his former vice-president, Walter Mondale.

Remember the fall of 1980, when Jimmy Carter was the
Democratic nominee and Ronald Reagan was the Republican
presidential candidate? That year the big issues were the
economy and inflation, the size and spending of the federal
government, and the condition of our national defense. On
each of these issues, more voters agreed with the Republican
challenger than with the Democratic incumbent. So the
Carter folks, having essentially lost the debate over the message, decided to go after the messenger and raise questions
about the ability of Ronald Reagan as well as about his com-
passion and intellect. The basic message of the Carter campaign became "Our guy may be no day at the beach, but
the other fellow is no month in the country."

Well, this time it appears that the game plan of the
Mondale folks is to paint Senator Gary Hart as either un-
stable, unknown, or undependable. It would appear that

Hart has already won the argument about the future, and Mondale would just as soon not debate that point any more. Hart's message has triumphed. Now the Mondale people hope to discredit Hart the messenger. It will be interesting to see if the strategy works better for Mondale in 1984 than it did for Jimmy Carter in 1980.

* * * * *

To understand where the huge federal budget deficit came from, it is necessary only to recall the three basic questions of the 1980 campaign and to be more or less familiar with those wonderful tabloid newspapers on sale at grocery store check-out counters.

In 1980, a bunch of questions were asked of American voters. And three simple solutions were offered. Is double-digit inflation absolutely pernicious and unacceptable? Yes. What causes that inflation? The federal government with its policy of unbalanced federal budgets. That's who. Solution: Balance the budget.

Are we tired of being pushed around in the world by a zealot like the Ayatollah, holding fifty-two Americans and our entire nation hostage? Of course we are. Solution: Let's double the defense budget.

What about your taxes? A little high? Has inflation boosted you into higher-bracket creep? Definitely. Solution: Let's cut everybody's taxes by a third.

Now, think about those tabloid papers on sale at the grocery store check-out counters—you know, the ones with the story datelined Chilicothe, Ohio, about somebody's brother leaving last Thursday on a UFO. These tabloids invariably picture somebody with an eighteen-inch waist who says she lost thirty-three pounds in three weeks on a diet of unlimited Hot Fudge Sundaes.

What we had in this country over the past three years was the economic equivalent of a Hot Fudge Sundae Diet: How do we pay for doubling the defense budget and standing tall? We cut taxes by a third. And what about that balanced federal budget we discussed earlier? Come on, don't be a wet blanket . . . all the savings and investment, as a direct result of the tax cut, will produce thirteen million new jobs eventually and those thirteen million will pay taxes (albeit at a reduced rate) and eventually the budget . . . will . . . be . . . balanced. Just like Hot Fudge eats calories.

April

Apr. 3 . . . Mondale wins New York primary; Jesse Jackson carries 87% of the black vote. Apr. 10 . . . Mondale easily wins Pennsylvania primary. Apr. 25 . . . Mondale drops labor-financed PACs supporting his delegates. Apr. 27 . . . Mondale announces he will return PAC money. Apr. 26–May 1 . . . Reagan visits China on a "Journey for Peace." Apr. 30 . . . Hart attacks "tainted delegates"; questions Mondale's control of campaign.

"NOW WHAT? THE GUY I DECIDED TO VOTE AGAINST DROPPED OUT!"

*I*n American politics we sometimes pigeonhole people by the cars they drive. For example, the typical John Anderson voter of 1980 was supposed to enjoy white wine and French cheese and drive a Volvo. That was the stereotype. Now we have a 1984 survey of people who actually drive foreign cars and how they voted in the Massachusetts primary: 3 percent for Jesse Jackson, 9 percent for John Glenn, 15 percent for Walter Mondale, 26 percent for George McGovern, and a full 45 percent of foreign-car owners for Gary Hart. Better than seven out of ten for either Hart or McGovern. Maybe there is something to that stereotype. Maybe, in the politics of 1984, we are what we drive.

*   *   *   *   *

Washington has been accused of being a somber city of student-body presidents always putting their best foot forward. But our capital city is not always full of self-seriousness. Every spring the press corps, through a group called the Gridiron Club, puts on a dinner, where in songs and skits they tweak the powerful, including whoever happens to be president of the United States. Last Saturday night's Gridiron dinner included some funny lines, proving that Washington does have a sense of humor, sometimes.

Bob Strauss, the former Democratic national chairman, represented the Democrats at the 1984 Gridiron dinner. Here are some of his lines that drew laughs from the crowd, including President Ronald Reagan. Said Bob Strauss, who is Jewish, "Let's relax and enjoy ourselves. So what if the program is running a little late, Mr. President. We are two guys who don't have to get up for church tomorrow." "Of course, when they separated Jim Baker and Ed Meese, the only Administration team left in town was Evans and Novak." "I understand," said Strauss, "that when they were discussing the Middle East at the White House someone mentioned the West Bank. At which point Ed Meese said, 'Don't look at me, I don't owe them a nickel.' " Strauss had this needle for the sudden rise of Senator Gary Hart. "The Democrats seem to be following the advice of that great political philosopher, Mae West, who said, 'When I am forced to choose between two evils, I always choose the one I haven't tried before.'"

* * * * *

Pennsylvania is politically not New York, which ought to sound like good news to the Gary Hart presidential campaign. The state's Democratic electorate is not so easily divisible into constituencies (other, perhaps, than labor and non-labor) as is New York's. New York Democratic voters are much more self-consciously and aggressively ethnic and religious than their counterparts in Pennsylvania, where a more blue-collar electorate's concerns run to the economic—jobs, the price of housing and medical care—which may not be bad news for Walter Mondale.

As the candidates work Pennsylvania, a state that is hurting with an unemployment rate one-quarter higher than that of the nation, the race between Mondale and Hart seems to have been defined at least for the time being. Democratic voters, not unlike other Americans, are looking for a couple of basics in a 1984 president: an individual of established character and integrity who can be, at the same time, an instrument of change and improvement.

Now, barely five weeks after New Hampshire, Democratic voters—with the strong urging of Mondale and his advertising—seem to be expressing doubts about how well they know Gary Hart or grasp his brand of change. Questions persist about the specific content of the change the Coloradan champions and the full content of his character.

In New York, the state that provided America with its model for the contemporary welfare state, Mondale was able to exploit Hart's alleged switches on issues to feed suspicions about his steadiness and dependability, two qualities most people prefer their presidents to possess. Thus, in New York, Mondale's generally predictable and unswerving liberalism—which had earlier tagged him as the candidate of the past—was transformed into a character reference.

Hart suffers right now from having come too far too fast.

He needs a "history" and believable anchors to the present—a dose of innocence by association.

* * * * *

One Pennsylvania problem for the Hart campaign is that in the beautiful suburbs of Philadelphia, the great majority of the beautiful people who live there are George Bush Republicans, not George McGovern voters in '72 or John Anderson supporters in '80. Pennsylvania is not a culturally liberated place with a laissez-faire attitude toward unorthodox life styles.

In western Pennsylvania—around Pittsburgh—traditional values still thrive, with low divorce rates and more full-time housewives and mothers than in the rest of the nation. It is no accident that the local sports heroes there—Franco Harris of the football Steelers and the now-retired Willie Stargell of the baseball Pirates—embody the blue-collar virtues of sweat, strength, and determination. New York, by contrast, had Joe Namath and Reggie Jackson.

Pennsylvania is not loaded with the Yuppies (young, upwardly mobile professional types) who have flocked to the Hart candidacy in other places.

Hart's mission is clear, if not simple. He must persuade Pennsylvania Democrats that both he and his message of change are solid, thoughtful, and full of content, and that Walter Mondale is too tied to the past to change, and a little mean to boot. That's Pennsylvania with five days to go.

* * * * *

Right now there is very little love lost between the campaign of Fritz Mondale and that of Gary Hart. Harsh words have been exchanged and not forgotten on either side. But don't rule out the possibility of a Mondale-Hart ticket emerging from next July's Democratic convention in San Francisco.

The vice-presidency is a much disparaged and much ridiculed office. But the reality is different: six of the last eight presidents—Roosevelt, Truman, Kennedy, Johnson, Nixon, and Ford—all first either sought or held the vice-presidency before taking over the Oval Office. The argument in favor

of choosing Hart is immediate and practical. Mondale has
won races in the three primary states where the highest proportion of workers are union members: New York, Michigan,
and Pennsylvania. But Hart has won the three 1984 primary
states (Connecticut, Massachusetts, and Vermont) with the
highest proportion of college graduates. Even in Pennsylvania, where he was creamed, Gary Hart still solidly carried
all voters under the age of forty and college graduates. When
the time comes, and if Mondale is the nominee, Gary Hart
could make an awful lot of sense as a running mate—and it
could make sense for him to accept the offer.

* * * * *

TO: Gary Hart
FROM: Mark Shields, *Washington Post*, April 1984

Let's be candid: Three more weeks like the last three—
Illinois, New York, Pennsylvania—and we can all repair to
the nearest fern bar, there "to grapple with the painful
process of personal growth" over a Perrier Light. The sit-
uation is grave, but redeemable. However, you must act
immediately.

Do Accept Responsibility for What Has Happened. Your
battlefield conversion (after Walter Mondale's needling) to
support for moving the U.S. embassy in Israel to Jerusalem
was singularly unhelpful. It looked a lot like vote pandering
New York-style and persuaded many disappointed admirers
that you were, after all, just another "pol." Blaming the re-
sulting flap and other missteps on your loyal aides just com-
pounded the negative. It wasn't presidential.

*Do Forget 1988: Do Not Rule Out Vice-Presidency this
Year.* Recall Jerry Brown, whose remarkable string of victories in the late 1976 primaries dazzled the political world.
By 1980, presidential candidate Brown sparked about as
much excitement among Democrats as the news that the city
of Toledo would hold its own quiche bake-off. This could
be your best and only shot at either nomination. That's one
more than most candidates ever get.

Do Re-establish Your Differentness. You cannot compete
with Mondale in the art of constituency politics. He will beat

you every time, as he did on the embassy-transplant issue in New York. Your earliest success was attributable largely to the voter's perception that you were not a traditional tell-'em-what-they-want-to-hear candidate.

One bright spot in New York was your proposal—made on Wall Street—to limit the deductions for the chablis–lobster salad business lunch to just 70 percent and to use the Treasury revenues thereby collected for full funding of school lunch and child nutrition programs. That was a graphic way of demonstrating that the United States already has a "federal lunch policy" for both groups—schoolchildren and stockbrokers.

Treat Mondale and Jackson Alike. Tell voters where you disagree with Jackson on an issue. Both you and Mondale have been excessively deferential toward Jackson, which is how too many white liberals treat too many blacks.

Use the Education Issue. Force Mondale to defend one of his special interests, the Teachers' Union. Mondale argues the solution to the crisis in public education is more money. Reagan's answer to declining test scores is to put more chapel in the classroom. Both are wrong, and you can lead the way by insisting we need competency testing for all teachers (which the union opposes) and better pay for better teachers. Hang in there.

* * * * *

In California, politics is different. Just two years ago California, the state that has given the nation much (including the freeway, the drive-in restaurant, the hot tub, and self-assertiveness training), had the following statewide officeholders: a young bachelor governor who dated a rock star and flirted with Zen Buddhism; a senator who was a seventy-six-year-old Japanese-American semanticist and had been elected by defeating the son of the former heavyweight boxing champion.

The big daddy of all primaries is the Golden State on June 5 with its prize of 345 delegates. And while Gary Hart is given a very good chance of winning this huge prize, winning the California primary hasn't meant much in recent presidential nomination fights. Take 1980. The big fight was the Democratic primary that year. Who won California? Ted Kennedy did. In 1976, the winner of the California Democratic primary by over 1.2 million votes was not Jimmy Carter, the man who was nominated, but Jerry Brown. That same year, Jerry Ford won the Republican nomination but Ronald Reagan won the California primary. California has given us a lot of trends but very few nominees.

* * * * *

For forthrightly proclaiming—at least three times daily, whenever they were within the 212 area code—their pledge to transplant the United States embassy from Tel Aviv to Jerusalem, former Vice-President Walter Mondale and Senator Gary Hart were accused, by the scolds and the naggers, of fevered fawning before Jewish Democratic voters in New York.

Most realists understand that Mondale and Hart are not giant panderers; they are alert candidates merely being "responsive" to the concerns of potential constituents. As the nomination struggle continues, more responsiveness will undoubtedly be seen. There remain, to name just a few, primary and caucus campaigns in Texas on May 5, North Carolina and Ohio on May 8, and California and New Jersey on June 5. Just consider the possibilities.

May 1, San Antonio — Senator Hart admitted that, although he had seemed to say "now is the time to *forget* the Alamo," what he meant was that "remembering the Alamo is not a new idea." Hart branded as an affront to Mexico Mondale's vow to move our embassy in the country to El Paso, and instead called for multiple embassies in Austin, Forth Worth, Galveston, Houston, and San Antonio.

May 5, Raleigh, North Carolina – Promising "before the end of this decade to put America behind a safe cigarette," former Vice-President Mondale called Gary Hart's opposition to a federally funded crash project to produce "a healthy smoke," "nothing more than elitist snobbery." Mondale cited several studies which showed that smokers came from the ranks of blue-collar America. "Those coughs you hear are Democratic coughs," said Mondale.

May 6, Cincinnati — A Mondale spokesperson said the campaign would not make an issue of the discovery that Mr. Hart had *four* library cards in 1961: one in the name of Gary Hartpence, born 1936; another in the same name, born 1937; and Gary Hart cards for both years but with different signatures. Mondale meanwhile reaffirmed his support for the moving of our embassy in Prague to Cleveland.

June 1, Carmel, California — Standing in an American-made warm-up suit and domestic-content sneakers, Walter Mondale reminded a gathering of tanned and flat-tummied Californians that "I am a Scandinavian and the sauna is a Scandinavian tradition."

June 4, Atlantic City — Saying he welcomed the endorsement of the Amalgamated Croupiers and Bouncers Union, Walter Mondale quipped that Gary Hart "thought a Jacuzzi was a congressman from New Jersey." Hart, taking the Mondale needle seriously, said the only reason he had thought that was because of a staff foul-up since corrected by bringing a senior adviser on board. To divert attention from the controversy, Hart called for withdrawing all U.S. troops from the New England states.

May

May 1 . . . Jesse Jackson wins D.C. primary; Mondale victor in Tennessee. May 2 . . . Reagan meets with Pope John Paul II in Alaska. May 5 . . . Jackson wins Louisiana primary; Mondale wins Texas precinct caucuses. May 8 . . . Hart wins Ohio and Indiana primaries; Mondale wins primaries in North Carolina and Maryland. May 9 . . . UPI gives Mondale commanding delegate lead (1,518 of 1,967 needed). May 15 . . . Hart winner in Oregon and Nebraska primaries.

*I*n 1984, some six months before Election Day, a growing number of Democrats are sustained only by the hope that, sometime this fall, the incumbent president will slip and "do something"—make an outrageous blunder or suffer a serious political setback—that will turn things around and produce a Democratic victory.

Loyal supporters of Walter Mondale, many of whom have always been frank to admit he would be a distinct underdog against Ronald Reagan, are now acknowledging their pessimism about the fall campaign. As one Mondale supporter put it the other day: "I used to think it would only require Reagan's catching a cold in October. Now I'm afraid it's going to take his contracting amnesia the same week he mistakenly says that Minneapolis is the capital of France."

The immediate cause of the outbreak of melancholia among the Mondalians was the injury to Mondale by the disclosure—and the way it was so arrogantly and ineptly handled by the Mondale campaign—that some 128 allegedly independent delegate committees had collected a couple of hundred grand from political action committees belonging to labor unions. This news was complicated by the fact that in February 1983 Mondale had joined Gary Hart in pledging that he would refuse all contributions from PACs to his presidential campaign.

Scratch a couple of potentially useful themes for use against Ronald Reagan in the autumn of '84. Mondale had gotten some response from his charges that Reagan was detached from what was going on in his own administration and that what was going on too often revealed an indifference to high ethical standards—the so-called "sleaze" factor. Now it appears that Mondale either did not know or could not control what was going on in his own campaign concerning PAC contributions to his delegate committees. Talk about detachment.

The fact that the delegate committee contributions were overwhelmingly from labor PACs revives the Is-Fritz-His-

Own-Man? issue, which it seemed, after his fighting comeback from the New England defeats, Mondale had mostly
overcome. Labor itself seems to grasp better than the Mondale campaign that labor support can be a liability.

Right now there is hardly a Mondale supporter, other than
those dedicated souls working seven days a week in his campaign, who can offer a semi-plausible theory on how the
Minnesotan can "win" the fall race. All game plans concen-
trate on how Reagan can "lose" instead.

The perception that major mistakes by Reagan are the best,
and possibly only, route to the White House can dictate a
campaign strategy with a single objective—to provoke a major
misstep on the part of the incumbent. This could mean a
most unorthodox campaign plan in everything from the selection of a running mate to debate strategy and agenda.

* * * * *

As a dues-paying member of the unofficial fraternity of
political sages, pundits, and other assorted wise men, I want
to launch a formal protest over the results in Ohio yesterday
and from Texas last Saturday.

Even a rookie political pundit could have told you what
was going to happen in the Democratic presidential races
in Texas and Ohio. First you had the front runner, a labor-
liberal protégé of Hubert Humphrey, with the endorsement
of the AFL-CIO, the teachers' unions, and the Speaker of
the House, running against the maverick Colorado senator
with a distrust of big government, sporting his cowboy boots
and emphasizing his western roots. So what happens? In
Texas, the western state where big oil gets its mail, the
candidate of the AFL-CIO and the teachers' unions wins in
a landslide. Then on to Ohio, the state with the second largest
number of United Auto Workers. Here the Westerner was
repeatedly attacked for his Senate vote against the Chrysler
bail-out, but in blue-collar Ohio, the mother of presidents,
the unexpected happened again and the Westerner won.
Twice in seventy-two hours the conventional wisdom was
dealt a serious blow. Believe me, it's enough to make a

pundit humble, or at least make him restate that most elementary of all political rules, namely, winning is still coming in first.

❋ ❋ ❋ ❋ ❋

Political speakers seem to be forever bragging that *their* party has members from every social, ethnic, religious, racial, and economic group. But that's not the way they put it. Their party, they boast, appeals to people "from all walks of life."

Nobody, of course, knows precisely how many walks there are in American life. The Bureau of Standards does not keep a list. But in Cleveland, during the recent Ohio primary, I saw at least a representative sampling of walks. Just about every campaigner in both parties has mastered the confident stroll, while most losing campaigns are still plagued by the unexpected stumble or trip, both of which frequently follow the candidate's clumsy attempt to tiptoe around a difficult issue.

The swagger was enjoying a comeback in popularity just as the stagger has receded with the advent of white wine. All candidates have to know how to march, but the slink seldom comes in handy. And only folks in the *other* party ever lurch or skulk. Never strut before election day is a pretty good rule. And the amble is still far more widely accepted than the mince, the prance, or the shuffle. Walking Tall is a favorite of the Reagan administration even though nobody has ever admitted to Walking Short or to "taking a walk"—on your friends or on your party, which is bad.

We're on the way to California where you can find Americans with a variety of interesting walks like the lope, the bolt, and the flounce, and where you can be sure that neither candidate expects to win in a walk.

❋ ❋ ❋ ❋ ❋

1984 had been scheduled to be the election year of the Great Realignment, when the Republicans would be elevated to their inevitable, if much-postponed, position as the nation's majority party. There will be no Great Realignment in 1984. It is not being predicted and it will not occur. The

Great Realignment was a casualty of the congressional campaign of 1982—which may turn out to have been a genuinely historic election, for both parties.

In 1982, an acute recession and some slick Democratic strategy combined to put Republican congressional candidates on the defensive. Democratic speeches—attacking the heartless, uncaring Republicans and their country-club indifference—were dusted off. One reason they worked was that the nation was then suffering from the highest unemployment since Pearl Harbor; the other reason was that the Democratic Speaker of the House had outflanked the White House in determining the dialogue of that campaign. 1982 was the year when virtually every Republican candidate had to testify daily that he was committed to the preservation of the Social Security system and that he would do whatever Representative Claude Pepper wanted to save Social Security.

Republicans, including the president, have never fully recovered from that campaign. They defensively insist that they are not heartless, cruel, and uncaring. To prove their point, they say things like "we have increased the total number of people who are getting food and the total number of dollars we are spending on food stamps" or "we're feeding more people who need help and nutrition than ever before in history." As long as the argument is about which party is more committed to spending public money to feed the hungry and to provide shelter for the needy, the Democrats will almost surely win. The quotes are the words of the current Republican president who, before the campaign of 1982, had never been accused of being "soft" on food stamps. In the campaign of 1982, Tip O'Neill stole the Great Realignment.

* * * * *

After his upset victory in the Ohio primary, Gary Hart is politically alive again. For the first time in twelve years the California Democratic presidential primary will be important. If the political press is composed of anything but chronic ingrates, then Hart, for justifying the press's attendance at Happy Hour in the Polo Lounge of the Beverly Hills

Hotel, ought to be the beneficiary of a few kind paragraphs. Hart also won a reprieve of sorts. Before Tuesday night, his options were both limited and unattractive.

Hart had not won a primary since Connecticut. And that was in March. Somewhere along the way he had seemed to lose both his voter appeal and his campaign theme. There was no overriding issue to carry him to the convention for a floor fight on the platform. Between Connecticut and Ohio, Gary Hart had become, in the cruel argot of his business, the political equivalent of the great First Date whom no one was asking to go steady.

The comeback enables Hart to postpone that awful reckoning he must eventually face with the conservative Colorado electorate that reelected him by just 19,000 votes in 1980. Constituents can be slightly perverse when a home-state product seeks national office. There is often real ambivalence—a sometimes lethal mixture of pride and resentment. Representative Morris K. Udall of Arizona nearly paid with his House seat after his 1976 presidential bid. Hart, who did well to win in the GOP year of 1980 without ever denying he was a national Democrat, represents a state where, in the last four elections, the Democratic presidential candidates have averaged 38 percent of the vote.

*   *   *   *   *

The heavy schedule of primaries on June 5 means that the presidential candidates and their traveling staffs will be spending more time on their chartered planes, where they and the press who are covering them are guaranteed to get more often in each other's way and on each other's nerves. This is the time and the setting when all political campaigns, in dealing with the press, resort to their version of evasion through intimidation.

Like other grown-ups and adolescents, political reporters suffer from bouts of insecurity. They, like foreign correspondents, assume some of the mannerisms of those they cover. For the foreign correspondent, that can mean a preference for raincoats with a surplus of belts and epaulets and what seem like their own vertical-hold buttons. For the political reporter, it means winning acceptance from the tough-minded politician for being "tough-minded." What reporters most fear is having their inquiry disparaged as too academic or abstract by a candidate's practical-minded political advisers. Such advisers, when they do not wish to discuss a subject, use the ultimate weapon of ridicule to silence the insecure reporter: "That's an inside-the-Beltway story."

The beltway in question is the circumferential highway around Washington. Virtually all of the Washington press live "inside the Beltway," but if a story is "inside-the-Beltway," it has nothing to do with the real world where people know the price of hamburger and Joe Lunchbucket stops after work for a shot and a beer. Every campaign has, by custom, a principal intimidator who delivers the inside-the-Beltway judgment to the offending reporter, often doing so with an air of disappointment that seems to say: "And all the time I thought you were a tough-minded and realistic pol."

Among earlier stories that were initially trashed as inside-the-Beltway by those who did not want them pursued were: 1) people view President Reagan as tilting toward the rich and the powerful; 2) Walter Mondale is too close to many interest groups; 3) people will be curious why Gary Hart changed both his name and his age; and 4) Edwin Meese's missed mortgage payments may constitute an obstacle to his confirmation as attorney general.

In these final tense weeks, when difficult and indelicate questions about losing and money are being asked, watch all campaigns try to throw the press off an unwelcome trail with the inside-the-Beltway line. And you can be sure it will work more than once.

❋ ❋ ❋ ❋ ❋

Political campaigns divide all media into two categories: paid and free. "Paid media" is the advertising that a campaign produces and purchases to get the candidate's message to the voters. The thirty-second TV spot is a favorite form of paid media. Campaign managers prefer paid media because they are able to control their message—what is being said, when, and more or less to whom.

But when you're broke—as the three Democratic presidential campaigns basically are—it means relying upon free media, which means candidate appearances in uncontrolled formats such as radio and TV talk shows, where hostile and embarrassing questions are frequently asked.

This is especially true in shockproof Los Angeles where on Tuesday afternoon, a seventy-five-year-old widow in semigraphic detail confided to a radio audience slightly larger than Vermont the desires of her seventy-four-year-old beau. The mix of a tired and testy candidate with a privacy-invading host could produce a serious candidate misstep.

But if there's a mistake to be made in the California free media battle, don't look for Mondale to make it. The Minnesotan is a shrewdly cautious politician.

The importance of television to all presidential politics was proved again recently when Gary Hart beat Walter Mondale by better than two to one in the Oregon and Nebraska primaries, just as he did in the Idaho caucuses. Because the networks didn't broadcast "primary specials" after the late local news, Oregon and Nebraska never really happened. Hart's exceptionally one-sided victories didn't receive free media attention or provide his campaign with political momentum.

The rule is: no primary actually matters unless Dan Rather, Tom Brokaw and Peter Jennings make it so by working the graveyard shift.

Hindsight enables the author to remind the reader that Senator Hart, at a subsequent Los Angeles fundraiser, won a whole lot of free media when he cracked that his wife, Lee, got to campaign in beautiful California while he had to go to New Jersey where he "got to hold samples from a toxic waste dump."

* * * * *

Some practical advice for candidates: We, Americans, are supposed to like our presidents with Humble Origins, which used to mean being born in a log cabin. But what about the poor, little rich kid of whom we are seeing more in recent political years? These candidates who through no fault of their own were born wealthy are almost always accused of trying to "buy" their elections. Here's one suggestion for these beleaguered sons of privilege in rebutting the odious charges. First, assure us non-wealthy voters that you are only spending millions of your own money to ensure your "independence from the pernicious special interests." If your opponents continue the attacks upon you for spending from your own fortune, then assume a hurt expression and, with restrained outrage, say slowly and sincerely: "I deeply resent my opponent's slur upon the decent people of our state. I know them too well, apparently a lot better than he does. Because I know that the people of this state are too intelligent and too independent to be 'bought' by anybody. My opponent owes the voters of our state an apology."

John McGlennon is a full-time teacher at the College of William and Mary and an occasional congressional candidate who tells of the practical advice he as a rookie candidate received from one grizzled veteran of Virginia politics. The subject was the most proper and productive conduct for a political candidate marching in any of the dozens of Memorial Day, Fourth of July, Labor Day, and Columbus Day parades to which he is invited. The advice given to John McGlennon went like this: "Wave to the lawn chairs, always wave to the lawn chairs. People who think ahead enough to bring lawn chairs to parades and set up the chairs along the parade route are the kind of people who vote. Believe me." McGlennon did, and so should any candidate marching up or down Main Street in any Memorial Day parade.

* * * * *

The people of Boston, lacking humility, used to call their hometown the Hub of the Universe. When the *Titanic* went down in the Atlantic, one Boston headline reportedly read, "Hub Man Lost at Sea." That's called looking for a local angle on a big story.

The June 5 California presidential primary is a big story, getting national attention. But here in Los Angeles there is front-page speculation about the kind of local angle that can help street sales of local papers. The question is whether former California Governor Jerry Brown, the 1976 candidate of new ideas, will endorse Senator Gary Hart, the 1984 candidate of new ideas. My answer is No, and I have a story to explain why.

In the early fifties, Orval Faubus was elected governor of Arkansas as a racial moderate. Faubus defeated an ardent segregationist who quoted history and Scripture in support of the separation of the races. When federal troops were later sent to Little Rock's Central High School to enforce the desegregation order, Governor Faubus resisted and overnight became a favorite of foes of integration. The segregationist he had earlier defeated said of Faubus's notoriety: "Damn Orval hit the jackpot on my nickel." Could anyone really blame Jerry Brown for not wanting Gary Hart in 1984 to hit the jackpot on the nickel of a younger generation with new ideas?

June

June 1–4 . . . Reagan visits Ireland, family birthplace.
June 5 . . . Mondale wins New Jersey and West Virginia
primaries; Hart wins California, New Mexico, and South
Dakota. June 6 . . . Reagan commemorates D-Day at Nor-
mandy. Mondale claims majority of delegates; Hart says,
"Welcome to Overtime." June 7 . . . Reagan attends eco-
nomic summit in London. Mondale announces beginning of
vice-presidential selection process. June 11 . . . Hart and
Jackson urge changes in delegate selection process.
June 14 . . . Reagan says that he is willing to debate Mon-
dale. June 16 . . . Mondale meets with Geraldine Ferraro
to discuss Democratic platform. June 21 . . . Mondale begins
interviewing vice-presidential prospects: Tom Bradley on
June 21; Lloyd Bentsen on June 23; and Wilson Goode on
June 28. June 25 . . . Edward Kennedy endorses Mondale.
June 26 . . . Mondale and Hart meet in New York, "united
by a profound fear of a second Reagan term."

*T*elevision news reviews of the first batch of 1984 Reagan-Bush TV commercials were almost uniformly harsh and negative. Generally political commercials are criticized because they deceive or trivialize. But these were criticized more for their production values. CBS asked "whether American voters will tolerate the video-packaging of the president the same way that airlines, rental cars, and light beers are packaged." NBC found that the Republican ads "package the president like a soft-drink commercial" and portray "a storybook America . . . where people own their own homes and nobody is out of work." To the Cable News Network, the GOP spots were "dream-like" and represented a "slick, Madison Avenue version of what America should be." As is usually the case where the slamming of TV is involved, the newspaper criticism was even more severe.

Please put me down on the other side. The first Reagan-Bush commercials of the campaign met the most important test of political advertising on TV: While they stretched the truth, they did not break it. Americans, as the spots insist, *are* more optimistic than they were four years ago, and, yes, it is "interesting that no one, anywhere, is saying the job of president is too big for one person." What has been overlooked in much of the criticism is that campaigns and candidates, in their own advertising, are entitled to put forward their own best case. Critics have yet to fault Fritz Mondale for failing to buy expensive TV time to remind voters of the Carter-Mondale year of 1979–80, when inflation raged at a cumulative rate of 25.7 percent, just as Gary Hart has not been expected to purchase a half-hour of prime time to reminisce about his management of the 1972 McGovern debacle. Yet some in the press question why the Reagan managers did not include references to unemployment, Central America, or Marines in Lebanon.

To watch the spots is to conclude that Ronald Reagan is running for head of the nation that is the United States, while his Democratic rivals, to listen to them, are running for the position of head of the United States government. There is a profound difference. The commercials have been called overly sentimental by many in the press and the opposition, who seem to have grown uncomfortable in the company of displays of patriotism and public affirmation of the American dream. The TV spots reveal nothing about where Reagan would propose to lead the nation in a second term. But they say much about where he wants us to believe he has taken us in his first.

* * * * *

On Tuesday night, when he in effect won the 1984 Democratic presidential nomination, Walter Mondale frankly acknowledged that he will be far from the favorite in this year's general election: "And to Ronald Reagan, my message comes from Satchel Paige: 'Don't look back, somebody's gaining on you.'" You can be certain that, at this very moment, a speech is being crafted for Mondale to deliver at the Independence, Mo., home of Harry Truman, the patron saint of political underdogs. Beginning no later than this afternoon, Democratic speakers will discover dozens of remarkable similarities between Mondale and Truman. The campaign of 1984 against a heavily favored, overconfident Republican party, we will be told, looks a lot like 1948 revisited.

With just twenty-two weeks left, the campaign of 1984 seems to me to bear a striking resemblance to 1936, when the party that had been routed four years earlier chose to blame that landslide defeat on the unpopularity of the defeated presidential nominee.

What is most interesting is the reaction of the two parties to the crushing defeats, nearly a half-century apart. With characteristic introspection, the Democrats after 1980 concluded that the whole thing had been Jimmy Carter's fault. It seemed that nobody really liked the defeated president that much, that his self-righteousness contributed to the debacle. That was how many Republicans chose to analyze the 1932 results.

It is more comforting to be able to pin the blame on an uncongenial someone who was never "one of us." That also saves the party leaders from ever wrestling with the unpleasant possibility that, perhaps, the voters rejected "our" ideas and all of us. Roosevelt's 1936 sweep, when he won 523 electoral votes to Alf Landon's eight, suggested that the American voters had rejected more than Herbert Hoover's size-17 starched collars: The Republican ideas had been rejected and replaced by those belonging to the Democrats.

Of course, Americans still very much like and identify with underdogs, with which the Republicans have not recently been confused. But Ronald Reagan retains that most precious of political resources—good luck. It now looks as if interest rates may be on their way up, but it will be especially difficult for Fritz Mondale of the high-interest Carter administration to exploit that issue. The issue that Mondale used to defeat Gary Hart—the Minnesotan's experience—will be little help in the fall.

1936 or 1948? It could be either.

*   *   *   *   *

For 1984, the Democrats have adopted one crazy party rule that allows national convention delegates to follow the dictates of their conscience, and even to desert the presidential candidate under whose banner they were elected from their home state. It's an outrage, and it ought to be repealed.

If you or I or any other ordinary citizen runs for delegate to a national party convention, we almost always run committed or pledged to a particular presidential candidate. The voters are actually voting their presidential preferences—Hart, Mondale, Jackson, or Reagan—when they elect delegates. Very few voters are saying, "Hey, I'd really like to send old Mark Shields or Sally Sweetwater as a delegate to San Francisco or Dallas." A candidate for delegate is borrowing the most precious resource and valuable possession that any candidate for president has: his name. To somehow suggest that after I have been elected as a delegate pledged to Mondale, Reagan, Jackson, or Hart, I can have a Damascus experience that entitles me to abandon the candidate whose good name I used, is just unacceptable. Delegates ought to be bound to support the candidate to whom they were committed when they were chosen, and to do so until they are freed by that candidate. Delegates are there to express the will of the voters. It's as simple as that.

* * * * *

If the Democrats are to regain a majority in the Senate this election year, then their 1984 candidates will have to capture Republican seats in Illinois, Iowa, Mississippi, North Carolina, New Hampshire, Tennessee, and Texas. Each of the seven Democratic Senate nominees in those states is looking at Fritz Mondale's choice of a running mate to see how much of a drag—if any—the national ticket will turn out to be in November.

Tempering a genuine affection for Mondale on the part of most party members is the pervasive doubt about whether he can beat Reagan. Mondale has to change that pessimistic perception on or before July 19, the last night of the San Francisco convention. There are three intervening things Mondale must use to define himself and his candidacy: 1) whom he picks for VP, and how; 2) how firmly and fairly he handles his defeated rivals and unites the party; and, 3) the content and the quality of the acceptance speech he delivers. Of the three, of course, only the vice-presidential choice will be holding press conferences in Perth Amboy in October.

To this point, Fritz Mondale's eminently successful career has followed the established and celebrated route of performance, recognition, and reward. It may now be too much to ask him—in choosing a running mate—to do the totally unconventional and unexpected. But that is exactly what some of his loyal supporters are asking. While none of the seven Senate campaigns is denying they and Mondale have ever met, none is publicly clutching for his coattails either. As evidence of the difficulty of the Mondale choice, most Senate campaigns would prefer that he choose a running mate who would answer an indigenous problem, e.g., a local boy with solid defense credentials in the South or somebody with appeal to white ethnics and Catholics up North. But only one can be chosen, which brings us to the two most probable finalists: New York Governor Mario Cuomo and Arkansas Senator Dale Bumpers.

Mario Cuomo, not a longtime Mondale ally, was lukewarm in the period of the front runner's early prosperity, but became Mondale's most effective advocate in the adversity of March. Many potential Democratic deserters this year are ethnics, and more than a few are Italian-Americans who could be expected to support the first one of their own to be nominated for national office. But more important, Mario Cuomo is one of the very few elected liberals anywhere who is comfortable in the company of traditional values. When was the last time you saw a Democratic liberal pinning a citation for bravery on the chest of a cop without apologizing to the ACLU? Cuomo did last week.

But if Cuomo, an eloquent advocate of Democratic progress and values, does not, as those closest to him insist, want to run, then Dale Bumpers may be the best bet. Bumpers is equally eloquent, a true spellbinder on the stump and, like Cuomo, a man with an interesting and bright mind. The choice of Bumpers could be Mondale's declaration of independence from the big interest groups. After all, Bumpers voted against the AFL-CIO's labor reform bill and opposed the feminists on extending the period for ratification of the ERA. Choosing either man would indicate that Mondale is comfortable with himself and not fearful of being eclipsed by his running mate. It is a big and tough choice to make.

* * * * *

In what has to qualify as the single most candid statement in this presidential election year, a year of smooth talk and "no comments," Jesse Jackson answered the question of what he wanted from the 1984 Democratic convention and the party's likely nominee, Walter Mondale.

When Jesse Jackson was asked just exactly what he wanted from the leadership of the Democratic party, Jackson answered succinctly, *respect*. That's entirely believable. Like most of us, Jesse Jackson did not want to be taken for granted or to have his remarkable achievements forgotten. All of this made me recall the words last month of a Los Angeles postal

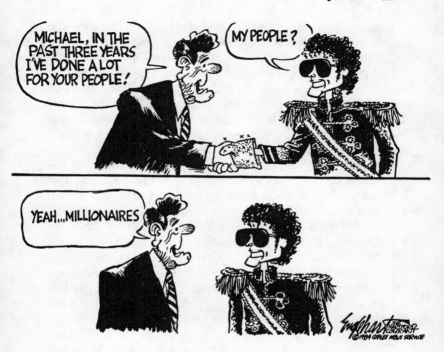

worker who explained why he intended to vote for Jesse Jackson in last Tuesday's California primary. The postal worker, a black American, explained that he had an eight-year-old son and that since Jesse Jackson had been running for president of the United States, that eight-year-old son had a new ambition. No longer did he want to be Magic Johnson, point guard for the basketball Lakers, when he grew up. Now, beamed his proud father, his son wanted to be president of the United States. Jesse Jackson made that difference for an eight-year-old black American. He deserves a lot of people's respect for what he has already done.

❋ ❋ ❋ ❋ ❋

The most cranky and impractical people in American politics all end up in the same place: writing the party platform for the Republicans and Democrats.

Right now most of the press attention has been on the Democrats' platform writing, and tensions present among the supporters of Fritz Mondale and Gary Hart and Jesse Jackson. You can't blame the Reagan White House for hoping that attention remains fixed on the Democrats, because even as we speak, some cranky and impractical Republicans are busy on their party platform committee trying to make the GOP more pure and the president's reelection more difficult. To rebut the popular perception that his administration cares more about the well-to-do than it does about the not-so-well-to-do, President Reagan in his last press conference told how under his administration more money is being spent on food stamps for the needy than at any other time in the nation's history. So what are a few true believers in the Republican platform doing? Trying to get language adopted that would offer federal assistance not to the truly needy, but only to the "very truly needy." In other words, reinforcing that negative stereotype of Republicans as uncaring and compassionless. It's just exactly what Ronald Reagan doesn't need from his platform committee.

*   *   *   *   *

Timing may not be precisely everything in politics, but without it, very little is achievable. This is something upon which a currently semi-reluctant Democratic vice-presidential possibility, New York Governor Mario Cuomo, may wish to reflect as he peruses the latest biography of "President" Nelson Rockefeller, who was shrewdly counseled in 1960 to wait for 1964, which was bound to be "a better year." As Rockefeller learned in 1964 and Jerry Brown, 1976's political rookie of the year, was to learn in 1980, the first chance was often the best.

Just as there is a tide in the affairs of candidates, so, too, are there undertows, heavy seas, and washouts. The American voter, who was eager in 1976 to discover in Jimmy Carter's aggressively non-ideological political virginity some high electoral virtue, was eager by 1980 to choose the minority party's ideological leader as president, at least partly because he was "not indecisive."

This year Mario Cuomo is a hot political property. The New Yorker's admirable ability to explain liberal Democratic programs in the natural language of traditional American values guarantees his warm welcome in a party plagued by self-doubt about its recent past and its immediate future. With the possible exception of the American situation-comedy, politics is probably our most imitative public activity. For that reason, by the first of October, every Democratic candidate will have adopted and burnished his or her own version of the Cuomo "Family" speech.

But in competitive politics, uniqueness has a short life expectancy. And staying "hot" for six years in New York cannot be done. Cuomo explains his reluctance in terms of a pledge he made during his 1982 gubernatorial primary race against New York Mayor Ed Koch to serve out a full term, if elected. The fact is that New York voters, like those in every state, are thrilled and flattered when one of their state office-holders is mentioned favorably for vice-president.

True, the child has yet to be born whose ambition it was to grow up to become either a lieutenant governor or a vice-president. But one thing to remember, in case you are asked to go to Minnesota for an interview, is that once you have run for vice-president, even if you have lost, no crotchety reporter will ever ask you four years later: Just why are you running for president? Timing counts, and the first time may turn out to be the only time.

July

July 2 . . . Mondale continues vice-presidential candidate interviews: Geraldine Ferraro on July 2; Henry Cisneros on July 4; and, Martha Layne Collins on July 6. Mario Cuomo and Dale Bumpers withdraw their names from consideration. July 12 . . . Mondale announces choice of Geraldine Ferraro for vice-presidential nomination. July 12 . . . Reported that Mondale plans to replace Charles Manatt with Bert Lance as chairman of Democratic National Committee. July 14 . . . Mondale announces that Manatt will be replaced but Lance will be campaign general chairman, not head of the DNC. July 15 . . . Agreement announced that Manatt will stay on at DNC. Cuomo delivers keynote address to Democratic National Convention. July 17 . . . Jackson delivers powerful speech to convention. July 19 . . . Mondale and Ferraro nominated; Mondale address cites "new realism," says he'll raise taxes. July 24 . . . Reagan denies he has "secret plan for tax hike"; Dole says tax hike possible. Reagan manager Rollins says, "Geraldine Ferraro may be the biggest bust politically in recent years"; Reagan says he won't touch remark with "a 10-foot pole."

Washington — I just had coffee with Tom Bradley, the mayor of Los Angeles. In choosing a vice-presidential running mate, Walter Mondale can go a lot farther and do a lot worse. And he probably will.

Tom Bradley is an American success story. His story began in the cotton fields of Calvert, Texas, where he was born sixty-six years ago. His parents were sharecroppers who, like a lot of other Americans before and since, sought and eventually found a better life in California. In Los Angeles, Tom Bradley won a track and football scholarship to UCLA. In 1940, Tom Bradley joined the Los Angeles police department where he served for twenty-one years. He went to law school nights and passed the tough California bar exam. He was elected to the Los Angeles city council, and in 1973 to the office of mayor. He has twice been reelected mayor of this, the nation's second largest and most ethnically diverse city. In 1982, Tom Bradley came within one-half of one percent of the vote of winning the California governorship in a state where 93 percent of the voters are not black, which happens to be Tom Bradley's race.

About the possibility of his being chosen for vice-president, Tom Bradley said, "I've never asked to be judged by my race." But he went on to add, "The message about the American dream could not be spoken more eloquently than by the presence of a black on the national ticket, not only in this country, but around the world." Tom Bradley says something good about all of us.

❋ ❋ ❋ ❋ ❋

San Francisco — "May our words be sweet," goes an ancient prayer, "in case later we have to eat them."

When Walter Mondale began conducting his very public interviews to fill the vacancy of his running mate, I was more than a little skeptical. For a while it did look like Mondale intended to talk to at least one of everything, except perhaps Agnostics for a Metric America or Teamsters against Preservatives. When Mondale announced Thursday in Minnesota that he had chosen Representative Geraldine Ferraro of New

York to run with him, I admit that I was knocked off my pins, and I further confess that I was impressed and moved by the televised announcement. Actually anyone who is either a woman or has a mother, a wife, a sister, or a daughter was probably moved too. Geraldine Ferraro's own father came from Italy to America with the same dream that moved millions of others to leave the familiar and the known to risk everything, to seek the chance to become something different in this the new world. I don't know what the end result will be for the election of 1984, but I do know that we will almost surely never have another national campaign without a serious woman candidate. Fritz Mondale and Geraldine Ferraro have made a difference.

*   *   *   *   *

Democrats are not the only ones holding their July convention in San Francisco. This week the ladies of the evening or the world's oldest profession or whatever euphemism you prefer are holding their convention here too.

They call their group Coyote, which stands for Call Off Your Old Tired Ethics, and they are holding a four-day business meeting here in San Francisco just one week before the Democrats arrive to do their business. Coyote's stated agenda is more straightforward than many political platforms. The call girls call for the legalization of their trade and an improvement in their social status.

As Delores French of Atlanta told the *San Francisco Chronicle,* "If we upgrade the status of prostitutes to the status of homosexuals, we will have come a long way." She has something there. After the Democrats adopt the rules compromise worked out by Mondale and Hart supporters, all future party committees will have by party law at least one member who is homosexual. In addition, the party will be required to have an outreach program to encourage the involvement of homosexuals in party affairs. There is no similar party requirement for reaching out to Italian Americans, Polish Americans or White Anglo-Saxon Protestants. Delores French, a thirty-three-year-old independent entrepreneur from Atlanta, knows something about contemporary American politics and culture.

* * * * *

Paul Jagger was past forty when he bought his first house in his hometown of Akron, Ohio, just after World War II. Nothing too fancy, the house was only two blocks from where he and Evelyn had rented with their two young daughters, Nancy and Mary Jane. And it wasn't that far from the Firestone Tire and Rubber plant where Paul Jagger worked nights to pay the bills and to put aside enough so that his two girls would someday be able, as he constantly told them, to "go to college, because nobody can take an education away from you."

1984 will be the first presidential election in fifty-six years that the Democratic nominee for president will not be able to count on the vote of Paul Jagger, who died at the age of seventy-six two years ago, long after he had proudly watched both his girls graduate from college. He loved the Democratic party even more than the Cleveland Indians, and he believed in it almost as much as he believed in America and the value of education. The Republicans were not the party for people who worked nights; the Democrats, and especially Franklin Roosevelt, were the people who were on his side. In 1948, the Indians, who won the World Series that year, were not his only winner. That November he won $100, a not inconsiderable sum, betting on Harry Truman against Tom Dewey.

But FDR was the most special of all. When Paul Jagger was dying, he asked his Evelyn for only one thing. On his simple headstone in Akron's Rose Hill cemetery, he wanted an inscription. No poetry, thank you, nothing from the Psalms, just this statement: "I Voted for FDR Four Times."

You have to wonder, as the Democrats head for their San Francisco convention, what happened to the party that had been such a major part of the life and the dreams of an American worker, husband, and father such as Paul Jagger.

Did success and the emergence of an affluent middle class spoil the Democrats? Lately they have become the party not so much of optimism and a brighter future, but the political crepehangers of our time. FDR brimmed with ideas and optimism and a sense of true moral outrage. Today's Democrats seem painfully short of all three. Maybe it's simply a different time with different problems when our national mission can only be understood if it appears on your home computer.

Whatever the explanation, it can be said of both Paul Jagger and his beloved leader Franklin Delano Roosevelt that they don't make Democrats like that any more. What commitment and faith and passion is summed up in that one straightforward epitaph: "I Voted for FDR Four Times."

* * * * *

San Francisco — It was said of Tom Dewey, in 1948, that he snatched defeat from the jaws of victory. Over the weekend, Walter Mondale snatched optimism from many Democrats here.

On Thursday and Friday, the story of Mondale's selection of Representative Geraldine Ferraro to be his vice-presidential running mate dominated the national political news. The press was mostly favorable and may have represented the longest sustained positive coverage Walter Mondale has received this year.

So what do the Mondale folks do? They push their good news story of unity off the front pages with a report that they want to dump Californian Charles Manatt as party chief on the eve of the national convention in Manatt's home state.

In trying to sack party chairman Charles Manatt and then backing off, Fritz Mondale created some bad impressions. Here are a few headlines from the nation's newspapers. The *Washington Post:* "Mondale Reverses"; the *New York Times:* "Mondale Yields as Other Democrats Prod the Candidate for Reversal"; the *Los Angeles Times:* "Mondale Backs Down"; the *New York Daily News:* "Fritz Flip Flops." "Yields," "backs down," "reverses," "bows," are not the kind of *action* verbs associated with most great leaders, including fighting Harry Truman who is remembered, among other things, for firing—and not rehiring—General Douglas MacArthur.

If someone had offered you 100 big ones to transform Democratic national chairman Chuck Manatt in twenty-four hours into a sympathetic, almost heroic figure, you probably would have said the task was impossible at twice that price. I know I would have.

The high command of the Mondale Express was able to do far more in just half the time at no cost—except, maybe, to Mondale's November prospects. Chuck Manatt, as a direct consequence of his being humiliatingly and cruelly fired, is on the verge of becoming a beloved and noble Democratic martyr. Just imagine what a Mondale campaign able to do all that for Chuck Manatt in only twenty-four hours might achieve for the candidate whose name it bears.

Democrats in the Moscone Center and elsewhere weren't laughing. No elected Democrats pretended to explain or rose to defend the Mondale sacking of Manatt and the plan to replace him with Bert Lance of Calhoun, Georgia, and the Jimmy Carter administration. Most everyone who knows Bert Lance likes him. But as one Democrat here put it: "To most people Bert Lance means two things: Jimmy Carter and kind of questionable bank loans." Mondale had not been seeking closer identification with either item.

The Lance-Manatt foul-up led to a rash of recriminations and very nearly to a fist fight within the Mondale campaign leadership. Add to this tension the anxiety generated by the campaign management's unexplained failure to offer any state assignments to their coordinators and organizers for the general election. All campaign workers everywhere are compensated in psychic income—appreciation, involvement, recognition, and a sense of shared mission. The Mondale state organizers were left in personal and professional limbo, bereft of psychic income or reassurance. As for the sense of mission, one Mondale worker confessed that the choice of Representative Geraldine Ferraro as a running mate had provided the Mondale "brain-dead campaign" with a sense of purpose that was needed even more than the sense of excitement it generated.

Most discouraging of all in the view of some Democrats who watched Mondale go eyeball-to-eyeball with Manatt and blink, was the realization that the Minnesotan's campaign is still very much wed—at least tactically—to constituent politics. Bert Lance was chosen at least partly as a bridge, or a sop, to white Southern voters, as though people, when choosing their president, actually care who the hell anybody's national chairman is or was. American voters choose their presidents for their personal qualities, which include decisiveness, judgment, fairness, and stability. The Manatt story may go away, but the impression will remain.

*   *   *   *   *

Let's face it. The Reagan administration has done almost as much for the balanced federal budget as Bob Guccione of *Penthouse* has done for good taste and the First Amendment.

At his Tuesday night press conference, the president, firm in his belief that repetition remains the first law of learning, insisted that he has the remedy for our mushrooming federal deficits—a constitutional amendment that would mandate a balanced federal budget. Coming from the same man who has yet to submit a budget anywhere near in balance in four years, this solution is a little bit like Bonnie and Clyde blaming their bank-robbing spree on the absence of a tough federal gun control law.

What we have here is a political role reversal. Democrat Walter ("Fritz") Mondale, renowned for his caution and for touching all the erogenous zones of the body politic, suddenly turns bold. He rolls the dice by picking Representative Geraldine Ferraro as his running mate. Then he tells the nation in his acceptance speech that, as president, he will raise taxes.

Next, Ronald Reagan, a genuine political insurgent, turns evasive and indecisive. He doesn't know about debates and says he has no plans for a tax increase. Then the president recycles the balanced-budget amendment, which died last year in the Republican Senate.

Nothing, however, has frustrated Mr. Reagan's critics and opponents more than the president's seeming ability to avoid nearly all blame and most responsibility for things that have not gone well. As one Democratic wit put it, "You get the feeling that if Ronald Reagan drove a convertible with the top down through a car wash somehow Jimmy Carter would get wet." This week, the president may have escaped getting soaked, but he was a lot more damp than dry. He was a candidate unsure about what to be proud of and unclear about where he wanted to take the nation he seeks to lead again.

*   *   *   *   *

On the question of whether the nation is ready for a woman vice-president, one region of the country is getting knocked unfairly.

Right after Representative Geraldine Ferraro's selection as Fritz Mondale's running mate, the wise ones—those with access to microphones and newspaper space—agreed overwhelmingly that somehow this meant the Democrats were writing off the South.

The assumption was clear. While the North and the West might be progressive enough to accept a woman in high public office, the South, with its fondness for mint juleps and crinolines, would not accept a woman candidate.

Wrong. The South has elected a lot more women to high public office than the trendy Northeast. Texas has had a woman governor. So, too, have Arkansas and Alabama. And today, the most popular officeholder in Texas may very well be State Treasurer Ann Richards, who has a lot to say about which banks get state deposits.

Florida has United States Senator Paula Hawkins, and Kentucky's governor is Martha Layne Collins, who was elected on the strength of her support among male blue-collar voters.

There is today no woman senator or governor in New York or Massachusetts, Minnesota or Wisconsin, or anywhere else in the Northeast or industrial Midwest.

Geraldine Ferraro's politics may not help her in the South, but her gender could be a lot less of a problem than up North.

August

Aug. 2 . . . Lance resigns Mondale campaign post.
Aug. 7 . . . Complaint filed against Ferraro with House
Ethics Committee over financial disclosure. Aug. 11 . . .
Reagan joke about bombing Soviet Union provokes criticism.
Aug. 12 . . . Ferraro says that her husband will not release
his tax returns. Aug. 18 . . . Zaccaro's tax information will
be released, Ferraro announces. Aug. 21 . . . Ferraro de-
fends her financial reports in press conference with 200
reporters. Aug. 23 . . . Reagan and Bush renominated by
Republican convention in Dallas. Reagan says at prayer
breakfast that religion and politics in America are insepa-
rable. Aug. 28 . . . Mondale and Jackson meet to avert rift
with black leaders. John Anderson endorses Mondale.

JOHNSON, YOU LOOK OUT FOR REPORTERS WITH RECORDING DEVICES...
SMITH, KEEP YOUR EYES OPEN FOR THREATENING INNUENDOS...
JONES, WATCH FOR SURPRISE QUESTIONS AND VERBAL ATTACKS..

*F*irst a prediction. John Zaccaro, the spouse of Democratic vice-presidential nominee Geraldine Ferraro, will sooner or later make public his income tax returns, and he will almost surely wish he had done so earlier and without reluctance.

Let's face it. Politically and journalistically, we are in uncharted waters. Nobody knows exactly how to treat the husband of a vice-presidential candidate. So far, Mr. Zaccaro has been spared the generally mindless questions to which political wives generally have been subjected: How do you keep your figure? Do you buy your suits off the rack or are they designer? Come to think of it, Mr. Zaccaro looks to be about a 40 regular.

But John Zaccaro, in order to give his wife even a fighting chance to win in November, is going to have to produce for public and press scrutiny his personal income tax returns. She promised them a month ago and then had to go back on that promise last weekend.

Since then, as she has campaigned on the West Coast, we have seen Geraldine Ferraro ducking questions about her husband's tax returns in California and Oregon.

It makes little difference that Mrs. George Bush's returns haven't been released and that in 1976 Mrs. Bob Dole's returns were not made public—or that Spiro (could I have the envelope, please) Agnew has yet to disclose.

For Geraldine Ferraro to get off the defensive, John Zaccaro will have to make his personal returns very public very soon.

* * * * *

Yes, there are differences and even tensions at this unified 1984 Republican convention, and most of the tension here is between the native-born Republicans and the naturalized Republicans.

Republicans can be divided into two groups: the native-born and the naturalized. The native-born Republicans are those whose parents and grandparents were Republicans, sometimes all the way back to Abraham Lincoln. From their ranks have come leaders named Lodge, Scranton, Bush, and Rockefeller.

But the story of this convention is of the naturalized Republicans, those who were born into Democratic families and chose to convert to the Republican party. Among the prominent naturalized Republicans here, all of whom were born Democrats, are Senator Strom Thurmond, Senator Jesse Helms, Texas Senate candidate Phil Gramm, and Rev. Jerry Falwell.

The more moderate native-borns have been elbowed aside by these energetic converts who have helped elect one of their own, an ex-liberal Democrat named Ronald Reagan, president of the United States.

Many of the native-born Republicans admit to feeling like strangers in the party into which they were born. Some of the newcomers openly encourage the early exit of those old-timers.

A Republican civil war, one between the naturalized and the native-born, is not out of the question in 1988 when George Bush, a native-born Republican who has wooed but not won the newcomers, is a likely candidate.

* * * * *

One of the things you and I should be grateful for today is that we do not have a brother running for president of the United States in 1984.

When somebody with a brother is nominated for, or worse, elected, president of the United States then immediately the press is all over that brother like a cheap suit asking all sorts of personal questions about what kind of a little kid the new president was and looking for some area of friction within the first family. And let's be frank, presidential brothers themselves have not always been any national treasure. There have been presidential brothers found using White House credit cards or making themselves available for hire to large public or private clients with large interests involving the U.S. government. To those clients, the qualifications of the presidential sibling appear at best to be very relative.

Which brings me directly to my nomination for the permanent first brother, regardless of who is president. My nominee is Neal Reagan, the incumbent president's older brother. Neal Reagan, who is retired, is not representing clients before the House Ways and Means Committee, or being handsomely retained by foreign governments. He offers no public advice on the running of the nation, no petty anecdotes about the president as a youngster. He is experienced on the job, he can take the pressure. That's why I nominate Neal Reagan for Permanent First Brother.

✸ ✸ ✸ ✸ ✸

In earlier, less sophisticated times, presidential nominees used to wait until Labor Day to begin their campaign. After watching the Democrats this August, I believe the old-timers knew what they were doing.

For generations the two parties would convene in the summer, nominate their national tickets and then the tickets and party leaders would spend the rest of the summer meeting and planning the fall campaigns, which would begin on Labor Day.

But this year the Democrats decided not to waste August and instead to spend the month campaigning against the Republican record. Undoubtedly, the argument for an active August went like this: Ronald Reagan is ahead in the polls. The economic news is good. The best hope for the Democrats would be for Mr. Reagan to make a mistake and show his age. If he's tired, he's more likely to make a mistake, and the way to tire Mr. Reagan out is get him campaigning early, in August.

So, what happened? The president jokes about bombing the Soviet Union. But that's elbowed off the front pages by the Ferraro and Zaccaro tax return story, the insensitive and inept separation of Bert Lance from the campaign, and the troubles with Jesse Jackson and Atlanta Mayor Andrew Young.

In the old, pre-media-consultant days, when the candidates took the month of August off to get their act together, the reporters would have been off somewhere, vacationing and

covering something else, and these flaps would have gone widely unnoticed.

Walter Mondale and Geraldine Ferraro now face a mission semi-possible. To understand the Democrats' formidable political task, it is only necessary to know the remarkably consistent answers in polls, over the last couple of years, to one question.

Here is a paraphrase of that *Washington Post*–ABC question: Which one of the following four statements most closely reflects your own feelings?

A. I like Ronald Reagan personally, and I generally agree with his policies.

B. I like Ronald Reagan personally, but I generally disagree with his policies.

C. I dislike Ronald Reagan personally, and I generally disagree with his policies.

D. I dislike Ronald Reagan personally, but I generally agree with his policies.

The results of this question have varied little since it was first asked in the spring of 1982. Only one out of ten respondents admits to disliking Ronald Reagan while approving of his policies (Statement D). Democratic Mondale activists come almost exclusively from the ranks of those who pick Statement C and find Reagan unlikeable and his policies disagreeable.

This leaves about seven out of ten voters who personally like Ronald Reagan, which probably comes as no great surprise. Of every seven Reagan-likers, four mostly agree with the president's policies, while three mostly disagree.

The good news from these results for Mondale and Ferraro is that half the voters mostly disagree with the president's policies and, therefore, might reasonably be expected to vote for his challenger.

The Democrats' difficult mission is to persuade voters who like Ronald Reagan personally that they can vote against his policies in November and still like him.

Mondale must reject totally the appeals and counsel of those who urge that the route to victory lies in just one more verbal bashing of the Gipper.

* * * * *

The current simmering debate about the president's shotgun marriage of church and politics reveals just how much the respective positions of the two parties have changed in only a generation. In the words of political thinker Bill Schneider, the Democratic party is now economically populist and socially and culturally elitist, while the Republicans are economically elitist and socially and culturally populist.

Throughout the political youth of Ronald Reagan, who voted four times for Franklin Roosevelt, the Democrats were

the more socially and culturally conservative of the two parties. The Republicans, especially the Northeast and Pacific
Northwest and Upper Midwest Republicans, were often the
more tolerant and accepting of social change.

If, only twenty years ago, a seer had predicted the emergence of legalized abortion in this country as a controversial
political issue on which the parties would polarize, very few
politicians would have prophesied that the Republican party
would be the anti-abortion party and the Democrats the pro-
abortion party. It is a good bet that the donors' list of
Planned Parenthood in 1964 was as overwhelmingly Republican as the Catholic vote that year was Democratic—three
out of four for Lyndon Johnson.

Perhaps there was no way for the Democrats to avoid becoming the gathering place for all the social-cultural activists
advocating women's rights, environmental protection, and de-
criminalization of drug use and deviant sexual behavior.
After all, the two great political and cultural battles of the
postwar era—civil rights and Vietnam—were joined and eventually resolved within the majority Democratic party. The
Democrats became the party to petition. Somewhere along
the way the leadership of the Democrats seemed to forget
how to say No to any alleged group with a socially "liberal"
cause.

But the Republicans, the traditionally tolerant party, have
courted the socially conservative voters with a vengeance
(sometimes unencumbered by personal beliefs or practices),
trying to fix the public debate on the social and cultural
issues, where they hope many "soft" Democrats live and vote.

September

Sept. 3 . . . *Labor Day campaigns officially begin.*
Sept. 6 . . . *Mondale attacks Reagan on religion and politics
at B'nai B'rith.* Sept. 15 . . . *Mondale shifts in staff, tactics
reported in* New York Times. *Sept. 16 . . . Gromyko-Reagan
meeting announced by White House. Sept. 17 . . . Debates
and format agreement set. Sept. 19 . . . Reagan courts Democrats at site of Kennedy speech in Waterbury, Connecticut.
Sept. 20 . . . U.S. Embassy bombed in Beirut; security questioned. Sept. 26 . . . Reagan delivers conciliatory speech at
United Nations. Gallup poll gives Reagan 57%-39% lead.
Sept. 27 . . . Mondale and Gromyko meet. Sept. 28 . . .
Reagan and Gromyko confer at White House.*

*I*t has been more than two weeks since any Republican officeholder of note has publicly criticized Geraldine Ferraro. The reasons for this moratorium have little to do with the good manners and charitable instincts of Republican party leaders. First is the fact that she and her husband did pay a hefty 41 percent of their income in taxes. Few politicians in either party probably pay that large a percentage so, rather than risk the embarrassment of having some nosy reporter ask, "Hey, what percentage did you pay, Mr. Party Leader?", party leaders have simply shut up.

The second reason could be called professional respect at the way Ferraro handled the hour-and-a-half press conference on her taxes. In the face of frequently hostile grilling, Ferraro kept her poise and answered the questions with facts and without self-righteousness or self-pity. No candidate for national office in either party in the last generation has ever proved he could have done any better.

Finally, the reason for silence is the lingering fear among Republicans that any unfair attacks on the first woman candidate for national office would be the catalyst to turn women voters to the Democrats in November.

* * * * *

TO: Fritz Mondale
SUBJECT: Winning

* Ignore all advice about wardrobe and/or cosmetic changes. The American voters, thank goodness, do not choose their president on the basis of his wardrobe or hairdo. If they did, Harry Truman's flowered sport shirts alone would have put Dewey in the White House. Remember these things: Every president, once in office, is guaranteed a place on Mister Phyllis's best-dressed list. In America clothes may make the man, but they don't make the president. Ronald Reagan owns and wears at least two suits that are the color of Gulden's spicy mustard.

* Forbid any more meetings about your "message." From the regular press reports about your campaign's series of eleventeen dozen meetings on the subject of what your "message" ought to be, there emerges one real message. It is, sadly, that after twenty years in national political life and after four years of running for president, you are somehow without a "message." The message is nothing more than forcefully expressing why you want to be president and how your presidency would differ most from that of the fellow who now holds the job. No more discussion on this subject.

* Ronald Reagan is the federal government; you, not he, must be the insurgent. As he began his reelection campaign, Reagan referred once again to the "puzzle palaces on the Potomac." This was a good line in the mid-sixties when Reagan first used it, but he—the man who has, for four years, selected the very people who run those "puzzle palaces"— cannot be allowed to run blithely "against" the very government he has headed. Whatever has happened in the executive branch since January 20, 1981, has been on the "watch" of Captain Reagan.

* Put on hold all the organized constituency groups that endorsed you. The key groups—the Birds 'n' Bunnies people, the Teachers Allied against the Testing of Teachers, and transvestite trade unionists—gave you their institutional imprimaturs and, presumably, their membership lists. And you can see how far behind you are today. Be civil, but they are not the route to victory.

* The route to victory begins with choosing one strategy and sticking with it. No more alterations or rolling readjustments. The choice is easy, because your options are severely limited. You must make specific, bold, dramatic proposals that keep the debate centered where it must be: in the Future.

* Do not attack Reagan directly, but use humor to needle him. In 1980, you used a line (until the Gray Panthers objected) that some Republican chairman was complaining about inflation and exclaimed: "This wouldn't have happened if Ronald Reagan were still alive."

The message in the humor must emphasize the president's perceived disengagement from his office. For example, the press likes to analyze every president's first hundred days in office; in Reagan's case, that milestone will be coming up in late October. Or, I always knew the president would run for reelection, because, as Mike Deaver admitted, Reagan left a wake-up call for 1984.

* Challenge us to be a nation and to be better than we are now. The message of the United States cannot be reduced to two selfish words: Me First. Jefferson wrote: "We mutually pledge to each other our lives, our fortunes, our sacred honor." Just as they, then, were in it together, so are we now. The question to be asked is: Are we better off than we were four years ago? Are the weak among us more secure? Are the strong more just? Americans will still respond to the call for shared sacrifice for the common good. Challenge us to a program of national service for all of us. Tell a powerful interest what it does not want to hear. You could begin by endorsing the loophole-closing Bradley-Gephardt Fair Tax bill and by doing it at a convention of Tax Shelter Executives. How's that for guts and fairness? You can do it. And wear whatever makes you comfortable. When you win, all America will be sporting red ties.

*   *   *   *   *

As everyone knows, young people (those between the ages of eighteen and thirty), unencumbered by the responsibilities of mortgages and families and still rebelling at older authority, are often quite liberal in their attitudes and their politics. But not this year.

Disraeli, the brilliant British prime minister and philosopher, may have put it best when he observed that any man who is not a socialist at twenty-one has no heart, and any man who is still a socialist at thirty-one has no head.

That has generally been the case in recent American politics. Young people, frequently fired with idealism, have been at the vanguard of liberal movements like civil rights. But this year, we are told, by margins of up to two to one young people between the ages of eighteen and thirty are enthusiastically backing the conservative candidate, Ronald Reagan.

Why the turnaround? One reason was given to me by, of all people, a Mondale press secretary, who believes that

"SORRY—I'VE DEPROGRAMMED MOONIES AND I'VE DEPROGRAMMED HARE KRISHNAS, BUT THERE'S NOTHING I CAN DO WITH 'YOUTH FOR REAGAN'!"

young people's attitudes toward politics and government are shaped largely by who was president and what government was doing when the young person first became aware of politics. The Mondale worker likes politics and has confidence in government, he explained, because John Kennedy was his first president and government was then doing something positive to achieve civil rights.

Now, it seems, young voters have two presidents to compare and evaluate: Jimmy Carter and Ronald Reagan. And they're picking Reagan two to one.

* * * * *

In 1984, Senator Gary Hart has already made his decision. If the current polls hold up and Ronald Reagan is reelected, this year's Democratic workers will not remember Gary Hart as a sulking spoiler, but more like a Ronald Reagan, whose own eloquent advocacy of Barry Goldwater in the latter's doomed 1964 campaign is still appreciated by Goldwater loyalists.

Hart, who was publicly indecisive about seeking or accept-

ing the vice-presidential spot on a Mondale ticket, admits
to no reservations about his preference for Mondale over
Reagan. We talked as he flew to California, after cancelling—
at the request of the Mondale campaign—a Labor Day trip
to Colorado.

Obviously altruism and party loyalty are not the exclusive
motives behind Hart's commitment of ten days to California
campaigning. Hart still has a large campaign debt to be paid
off and California is where a lot of Democratic contributors
and fundraisers live. Hart also knows that many Jimmy
Carter people resent Ted Kennedy's less than all-out commitment in the 1980 general election. There will be no legitimate
finger-pointing at Gary Hart in November or thereafter.

*   *   *   *   *

Democratic House candidates, less than seven weeks before Election Day 1984, are growing nervous. They, of course,
know that the happy days of Hymie Shorenstein are over.
What scares many of the Democrats is the fear that the un-
happy political fate of Gunn McKay may await them.

For those too young to remember, Hymie Shorenstein was
a Brooklyn Democratic leader who was renowned during the
New Deal for regularly delivering fifteen-to-one margins
from his district on election day. One party benefactor, whose
generosity had been rewarded with a Democratic judicial
nomination, became anxious as election day approached and
no billboards or brochures had appeared with his name or
likeness upon them. The concerned candidate was reassured
by Hymie Shorenstein, according to Theodore White (who
wasn't there either): "Listen, did you ever go down to the
wharf to see the Staten Island ferry come in? You ever watch
it, and look down in the water at all those chewing-gum
wrappers, and the banana peels and the garbage? When the
ferryboat comes into the wharf, automatically it pulls all the
garbage in too. The name of your ferryboat is Franklin D.
Roosevelt—stop worrying."

Gunn McKay was elected as a Democrat to the House from
Utah in 1970 and served five terms until his defeat in 1980.
In those ten years, Gunn McKay managed to survive 1976

when Jimmy Carter, at the top of the ticket, won just 37 percent of the vote in McKay's district, and 1972 when George McGovern lost McKay's district 77 percent to 23 percent. In 1980, Gunn McKay, in the First District of Utah, received 88,000 more votes than Jimmy Carter did, but McKay still lost while running some twenty-nine percentage points ahead of the Democratic president who lost the district to Ronald Reagan 77 percent to 19 percent.

What the most recent poll results guarantee is that Republican congressional candidates will be clamoring for joint appearances with or kind words from their Staten Island ferry, President Ronald Reagan. Democrats, in the words of one party strategist, "will be in the business of building huge wooden platforms" for visits from their nominee, so that local candidates will be able to testify they were on the platform while still being safely outside of camera range. Democratic candidates for House and local office will spend time, energy, and money explaining and emphasizing their differences with the national ticket, lest they suffer the fate of Gunn McKay.

Questions about bad poll results can turn even the sunniest of trailing candidates sour. But Fritz Mondale, who has seen more bad poll numbers than most juntas, this week came up with the best response of the decade when he said, "Look. The NBC poll on Sunday said we were thirty points behind. The next day on Monday, the Lou Harris poll said we were thirteen points behind. That means we've picked up seventeen points in just one day. At that rate, we'll beat Ronald Reagan by 107 points."

* * * * *

The Democrats have had a number of pretty good excuses to explain recent defeats. In 1968, the Democrats were split when George Wallace led a third party and Gene McCarthy sat on his hands. In 1972, George McGovern allegedly took advantage of the reform rules he had helped to write and captured the nomination. In 1980, Jimmy Carter, at heart an outsider, was trounced.

But Fritz Mondale is truly the Distilled Essence of the

Democratic party. Mondale was the endorsed candidate of organized labor and the largest teachers' union. Mondale was endorsed by feminist groups, environmental groups, and gay rights groups. Mondale was the choice of the Speaker of the House and of most Democratic members of Congress, at least those who had the guts to endorse a candidate. He was also the pick of major black politicians, and of leading Jewish and Hispanic politicians.

Now some of these same people criticize Mondale's campaign organization or speaking style. The facts are simple. If the Democrats lose big in 1984, it will almost surely be because, like the party's last four presidential candidates, Mondale will win only about 38 percent of the white vote. At some point, Democrats will be forced to conclude that as Pogo once put it, "We have met the enemy and it's us."

* * * * *

"Abortion." Just the mention of the word is enough to make elected officeholders break out into a cold sweat. And the reason is because abortion is an issue that leaves no room for what good politicians do best: Compromise.

On most political issues, even big differences can eventually be compromised by both sides giving a little. For example, if I believe fervently that the national minimum wage should be $7 per hour, and you believe just as devoutly that the minimum wage ought to be $1 per hour, then the chances are pretty good that we might be able to reach a compromise somewhere around $4 per hour or so.

But abortion does not work as a political issue. One side believes sincerely that abortion is the unjustified taking of innocent human life and the other side believes just as fervently that abortion is in many instances a medical blessing. There exists absolutely no possibility for compromise on the abortion question. What you have is both sides pressing their positions with greater intensity and with more passion. That's why most politicians who have sometimes been able to elevate compromise to an art form and a civic virtue so despise the political issue of abortion. There is no way a compromise can ever be reached on this most difficult, most sensitive, and most painful issue.

*   *   *   *   *

There's an old line that goes "Home is the place where when you have to go there, they have to take you in." For underdog Fritz Mondale, home on Wednesday was here in Cleveland among friends at the convention of the United Steel Workers of America.

There were no hecklers among the union steelworkers in the Cleveland Convention Center. No boos for Fritz Mondale. No unfriendly signs or banners to harass him. And Mondale brought the crowd to its feet several times with lines like "Both party platforms this year were prepared by Gerrys—ours was under the leadership of Geraldine Ferraro and theirs by Jerry Falwell."

But in tonight's TV news and tomorrow's papers, it will be one more appearance of Mondale, the union-endorsed candidate, playing to a union audience. Does that help close the large gap between the Democratic challenger and the incumbent Republican president? Probably not.

But there is a reason a candidate who is trailing chooses to seek out friendly crowds and preach to the choir politically. It's because candidates are human beings. They know when they are behind, and they realize there probably aren't that many votes to pick up by such a visit. But because they do have feelings, underdogs need to see some smiling faces and to hear some encouraging words and a few friendly cheers. That's the real reason why Fritz Mondale was in Cleveland on Wednesday.

*   *   *   *   *

On the West Side of Cleveland, ethnic blue-collar residents whose loyalty to the Democratic party once approached their loyalty to their neighborhoods and their parishes are now flirting again with Ronald Reagan and the Republicans. And there's a reason.

One of my favorite people in America is "Jimmy WestSide" of Cleveland. WestSide is obviously not his real name, but

Jimmy loves and understands the West Side ethnics or "cosmos" as they are called around Cleveland. Jimmy never left his native West Side. Here's how he explains the probable defections of lifelong Democrats to Ronald Reagan.

"You know, voting for a Republican once is a little bit like missing mass on Sunday for the first time. When the sky doesn't fall in on you, it's easier to miss it again a second time." Jimmy WestSide tells the story about watching the 1984 convention on TV at the bar of a veterans' club in Cleveland. The crowd was blue-collar by profession and Catholic by birth, mostly Italian, some Polish, and a few Irish.

As leaders of the various groups—feminists, gays, blacks, and Hispanics—appeared on TV making their non-negotiable demands and their threats to walk out, the crowd in the Cleveland bar looked on in a blend of amazement and disgust. One ethnic patron put it this way: "Hey, there's nobody there to walk for us." As Jimmy WestSide sees it, that's a large problem in 1984 for the Democrats among blue-collar voters. There's nobody there to walk for us.

October

Oct. 3 . . . Bush tax returns made public. Oct. 7 . . . First Reagan-Mondale debate in Louisville; Mondale widely viewed as winner. Oct. 8 . . . Mondale calls it a "brand-new race"; Laxalt calls it "an off night." Oct. 11 . . . Bush-Ferraro debate in Philadelphia. Oct. 12 . . . Bush evaluates debate performance as having "kicked a little ass last night." Reagan begins whistle-stop tour on Truman train through Ohio. Oct. 21 . . . Reagan and Mondale debate foreign policy in Kansas City.

"MISS JOHNSON, THIS COFFEE'S COLD.... ISSUE A STATEMENT BLAMING JIMMY CARTER."

*T*he format, as we have been told, precludes any genuine give-and-take between the presidential candidates. It is not so much a debate as it is a simultaneous press conference, with rebuttals. Yet the reality remains: Since 1960, televised presidential debates have three times profoundly influenced the American electorate's choice of a national leader.

In 1960 John Kennedy, disparaged as callow and inexperienced, blunted both charges in his first debate with Richard Nixon.

Sixteen years later, in the next presidential campaign where the candidates debated, incumbent Gerald Ford interrupted his own valiant comeback from a twenty-million-vote deficit to a virtual dead heat in that year's second debate in San Francisco by "liberating Poland."

In the 1980 campaign's only debate between the major party nominees, Ronald Reagan was not, as his belittlers anticipated he would be, exposed as either a fraud or a risk. Instead, by being avuncular and reasonable and by not advocating a personal nuclear device for every ROTC graduate, Reagan erased the mad-bomber image.

The impressions voters gain of the candidates from the televised debates are frequently lasting. In 1960, after watching the candidates debate on television, Marshall McLuhan saw Kennedy as a "shy, young sheriff" while Nixon resembled "the railway lawyer who signs leases that are not in the best interest of the folks in the little town." It's a good bet that the 1984 debates will influence the outcome of the 1984 election, too.

Ronald Reagan is to be commended for debating. In 1964 and 1972, Presidents Lyndon Johnson and Richard Nixon—incumbents with big leads in the polls—both ducked debates with their underdog opponents. In late 1979, after the takeover of the embassy in Teheran had transformed him from "weak" Jimmy to "strong" Jimmy and raised his poll numbers by close to forty points, President Carter pulled out of the *Des Moines Register* debate with Edward Kennedy and Jerry Brown before the Iowa caucuses.

By agreeing to debate, Reagan is providing his underdog challenger Walter Mondale with the largest crowd—maybe 120 million—ever to see and hear him. At the same time, Reagan is probably guaranteeing that his Oval Office successors will never again be able to duck a debate challenge from their opponents without looking like large chickens.

The challenger has a number of real advantages. For the first time in his own remarkable political career, Ronald Reagan may be overrated going into a showdown. After four years of being told what a gifted communicator the president is, few of us expect Mondale to get so much as a forensic first down. This is an advantage for the challenger, who is quick on his feet and bright.

Debates are "wholesale" events. Neither candidate can tailor his message to a specific group such as steelworkers or parents with children in parochial schools and tuition tax credits on their minds. Fritz Mondale will speak, courtesy of Ronald Reagan, to the most Republicans and independents who will ever hear him. At least until his inaugural.

Whatever else Mondale does on Sunday, he must speak to all of us at the same time, not as members of a professional or demographic group, but as Americans with an interest in our own and the nation's future.

* * * * *

For most Americans, no vote is more "personal" than the one cast for the presidency. We look for—and are confident we'll be able to detect—the special qualities of character, personality, and intellect we would most value that year in our national leader.

This year, American voters appear to prefer Ronald the Strong to Walter the Fair. His fellow citizens regard Fritz Mondale as more compassionate, peace-loving, and fair than Ronald Reagan. But Americans like their national leaders strong as well as sensitive, tough as well as tender. Time and again this political traveler is told by citizens who frankly acknowledge their disagreement with one or more Reagan policies, that they intend to vote for the president because "we need a strong leader." Nearly three out of four voters polled believe Reagan is a strong leader whereas a solid majority believes the Democratic nominee lacks strong leadership qualities.

Voters in September saw Mondale as a weaker leader than they had in July; they were undoubtedly influenced by the firing and re-hiring of party chairman Chuck Manatt, the hiring and semi-firing of Bert Lance, Mondale's semi break-up and make-up with Jesse Jackson, and the apparently conscious distancing of Mondale from Geraldine Ferraro—until she successfully passed the marathon press grilling on her finances. Throughout, Mondale never appeared to be the sort of strong, decisive leader who could, if necessary, bench-press NATO.

Offering no vision of the future, the latest Reagan TV commercials chose to run against "the past record of the Carter-Mondale administration." That's not totally unfair. But up to now, hampered partly by the surviving perception of Jimmy Carter as indecisive, the Democratic nominee is without a "strong" suit.

*   *   *   *   *

In the political jungle that Washington can be in the fall of an election year, there is one reliable test for determining which candidate won a presidential debate: In the seventy-two hours immediately following the debate, the winning candidate is the one whose previously unnamed advisers candidly, if bashfully, admit in the press that, yes, they were intimately involved in preparing their guy for the debate. Advisers for losing candidate-debaters are invariably more discreet. Just as in the fall of 1980 we learned that young David Stockman had brilliantly played the parts of both John Anderson and Jimmy Carter in Ronald Reagan's warm-ups, you can bet that this week we will be forced to meet the Mondale briefers.

Sometime before eleven o'clock EDT on Sunday night, October 7, Walter Mondale underwent an important public transformation. Before our very eyes, Mondale the Loser turned into Mondale the Underdog. This is potentially important, because Americans are funny people. While we alternately snicker or chuckle at losers, we root for likeable underdogs. After Sunday night, Mondale is no longer a wimp. He went toe-to-toe with our president and won a near-unanimous decision. In the colorful boast of his campaign pollster, "Mondale proved his mettle, while Reagan lost his Teflon."

Reagan spent most of the evening on the defensive, insisting that he was not the sort of fellow who delighted in throwing his disadvantaged contemporaries off Social Security. In the words of one Republican manager, the debate was "an unmitigated disaster for Reagan. The president did not look to be in command. He lost control of the agenda."

Reagan himself, with the selection of words before his closing statement, seemed to raise the age issue, which his halting performance is sure to resurrect in the campaign's closing weeks. In saying to moderator Barbara Walters, "I'm all confused now," Reagan used an adjective often employed to describe euphemistically the forgetfulness of older people.

By Monday morning, Democratic candidates and managers were smiling for the first time since the San Francisco convention. As one southern Democrat put it: "The mood is different. Mondale rehabilitated himself and Reagan is no longer seen as a superman who will carry on his coattails three dozen Republican House candidates." From a Republican manager: "There goes Chuck Percy," referring to the Illinois GOP senator, whose supporters had been counting on a strong Reagan effort to help the Foreign Relations Committee chairman survive against popular Democratic Representative Paul Simon.

While Mondale's performance was better than Reagan's, it was not unflawed. Still missing is any inspiring vision of challenge to Americans. But Mondale managed to be aggressive without being abrasive, while simultaneously conceding the president's immense personal appeal to voters ("I like President Reagan" should have made Mondale's nose grow three inches) and seeking to persuade Democratic voters to come home to their old party by pointing out that he, not the president, had worked for John Kennedy's election in 1960.

Once again the presidential debate has changed the conventional wisdom, if not the dynamics, of a presidential election campaign. The Reagan managers will now have to confront an electorate suspicious about their campaign strategy of keeping the president under wraps. Democrats will now be openly asking whether the presidential helicopter engines had been turned on so that the president could not be heard by voters.

* * * * *

In the past five days, to the surprise of a lot of his political admirers, Ronald Reagan has driven through two major political stop signs at about 85 miles an hour.

When he was shot in March of 1981, the president, upon entering the hospital, made everyone else feel better by saying, "I forgot to duck." That's an example of instinct, something you have to be born with. You can't learn instinct like the piano.

But last Sunday, Mr. Reagan's instinct in the 1984 debate was faulty. Despite warnings against doing so, the president tried to recycle his "There you go again" line from 1980. Mr. Mondale was ready, and his perfectly rehearsed rebuttal gave TV's most memorable moment of the evening. By Wednesday, everyone rooting for Mr. Reagan's reelection agreed not to talk any more about the first debate. Which means Mondale had won.

And then who brought up the question of Mondale's make-up somehow making a difference? That's right, that instinctive politician Ronald Reagan. Those two missteps have other politicians talking and watching.

* * * * *

George Bush, it turns out, suffers from the very same disability that has plagued Walter Mondale this entire campaign year: the "If You Only Knew Him in Private" virus.

All kinds of folks around Washington and politics will freely testify to what a terrific fellow Bush is in private conversation and personal encounters. But put him on display as he was in what could have been called the Valium-Dexedrine tournament in Philadelphia, and Bush turns excessive.

He is too happy with his assignments and in his work. And whatever good work he did Thursday night in interrupting the worst Reagan political week of the last two years was undone on Friday in New Jersey. There (in an aside to long-shoremen more than faintly reminiscent of Richard Nixon's eagerness to adopt what he thought to be the argot of his immediate audience) Bush used what he defended as sports vernacular to assess his debate performance. Those who had only seen the Philadelphia Bush could be forgiven for thinking the phrase began with "kissing," and not "kicking."

The lousy week included the up-to-now exemplary Mrs. George Bush scorning the Democratic vice-presidential nominee, Geraldine Ferraro, with a term that Mrs. Bush said she herself was too much of a lady to speak—but that rhymed with "rich." It didn't take Dick Tracy to figure it out after

Bush's longtime press secretary, Pete Teeley, called Ferraro "bitchy" in *The Wall Street Journal.* You have to wonder whether if Mondale had selected Texas Senator Lloyd Bentsen to be his running mate, the Bush entourage would have employed less gender-intensive epithets.

So the week ended with Bush back on the defensive. And that is where the Reagan campaign spent most of its time as well, especially on the campaign's big new issue: age.

But if the president's supporters had believed him to be more vigorous and more youthful than most of his contemporaries, then credit must be given to Reagan's own staff. After all, every presidential visit to California begins with those wonderful pictures of Reagan, in his non-designer work clothes, chopping wood or clearing brush from the trails of his ranch. There must somewhere be a pile of chopped wood big enough to keep every California fireplace toasty until 1990. Next the president is photographed riding his favorite horse—tall in the saddle, of course—on the very trails that he has made brush-free. Earlier there was the Oval Office picture of the seventy-three-year-old president arm-wrestling into submission some lumberjack with biceps slightly larger than an inflated basketball. This preceded the *Parade Magazine* cover showing the leader of the free world, stripped down to his T-shirt, pumping iron.

These photos, all conceived and produced by Reagan's chief aides, had only one purpose: to convince the American electorate that Ronald Reagan had found somewhere outside Santa Barbara what Ponce de Leon had spent all that time in Florida looking for. The "age" issue was introduced into the 1984 presidential campaign by Reagan's most loyal and prominent lieutenants.

❋ ❋ ❋ ❋ ❋

Cleveland, October 21 — Fritz Mondale started fast. He was out of the box with a blanket indictment of Reagan foreign policy of the last four years. The president was tentative early, and was forced to correct himself in his answer about the CIA assassination booklet in Nicaragua. But Mr.

Reagan gained his footing; when questioned about his age as a campaign issue, the seventy-three-year-old incumbent pledged *not* to make his opponent's "youth and inexperience" an issue in the 1984 campaign. It drew the intended laughs and smiles from the audience and seemed to give the president some confidence. After that, the shift was to Reagan and away from Mondale, who had needed a knockout to win.

* * * * *

Because we Americans insist on comparing each president with his predecessors, since 1945, every president has been compared—unfavorably—with FDR. But Ronald Reagan is probably the best-liked American president in at least twenty years. One reason for this is that Ronald Reagan is a man publicly free of self-pity; he doesn't spend time telling us what a tough, thankless job he has and how lonely and burdensome are the duties of the chief executive.

Former Vice-President Mondale has said that "Americans want a president who is engaged, not detached." Here Mondale could be making a mistake common to Washington where people frequently confuse input (that's hours spent) with output (results obtained). As president, Mondale's old boss, with his eighteen-hour days, gave hard work a bad name.

Mr. Carter and some of Mr. Reagan's other recent predecessors seemed to feel obliged to remind us regularly what selfless sacrifices they were daily making in our behalf. This was always unappealing, especially after most of them had spent much of their adult lives scheming to win the job they were, at that moment, complaining about. As usual, Senator Bob Dole, the Kansas Republican, doesn't mince words with his analysis of presidential predecessors. In describing a recent Washington dinner, where former Presidents Jimmy Carter, Gerald Ford, and Richard Nixon were in attendance, he referred to the three ex-presidents as "See no Evil . . . Hear No Evil . . . and . . . Evil." These are a couple of reasons why Ronald Reagan cannot be considered an underdog for reelection.

* * * * *

An argument some Democrats have tried to use mightily this fall to persuade voters not to vote for Ronald Reagan is that there's a very good chance the next president will appoint up to five new Supreme Court justices. It's an argument that has persuaded absolutely nobody.

Don't let Jerry Falwell appoint Supreme Court judges. That's what Democrats shout as they try to raise the specter of that conservative Virginia fundamentalist clergyman picking the next justices. Sorry Democrats, but that dog just won't hunt. Ronald Reagan has already made one Supreme Court appointment, and the nomination of Sandra Day O'Connor, in addition to making history, also made a lot of right-wing Republicans pretty darn angry. But even more important is the ABC News Poll that showed 49 percent of Americans worry a great deal or a good amount about having their home burglarized. For women, the figure was up to 55 percent who worried. And among black Americans, seven out of ten worried a great deal. For many concerned citizens, judges who promise to get tough on criminals, especially burglars, are more to be welcomed than to be feared.

* * * * *

You're Fritz Mondale, and the news lately has not been good. Yes, you probably "won" the Kansas City debate, but that, under the unpublished rules of political expectations, does not mean that Ronald Reagan "lost." By now you have probably concluded a couple of hundred times that last Sunday night you should have confronted Reagan by quoting from his 1960 letter to Richard Nixon in which Reagan—who this autumn has been all but canonizing John Kennedy—castigated the late president's campaign as "old Karl Marx." We'll never know just how badly Reagan might have stumbled on live, national TV.

But now the question is no longer what Fritz Mondale ought to have done; it is what he ought to do in the last ten days of what will probably be his last national campaign. What does he choose to say, and to whom? How can he give most help to other Democrats on the ballot and still preserve his now slender hopes for presidential victory? What does

Mondale want to say to posterity about what he stood for in 1984? How does he want to write his political epitaph?

These are hard questions for anyone to be asked, let alone to answer. But in the last two weeks of any campaign when a candidate trails his opponent by a margin (12 percent) three times larger than the undecided vote (4 percent), the possibility of defeat cannot be ignored. In the judgment of other Democratic campaigns that have been saddled this fall with their nominee's acceptance speech pledge to raise taxes to pay off the federal deficit, what Fritz Mondale ought to be saying is: "As president, I'll raise your taxes. And so will Ronald Reagan; make no mistake about it. He won't tell you. And I sincerely wish I hadn't." Mondale's convention candor failed to achieve its intended effect of keeping an evasive Reagan on the defensive. Instead, other Democrats have found themselves on the defensive, and Reagan has been able to make the issue into an applause line.

Mondale would accomplish nothing by throwing raw meat to his true believers in the form of more Reagan-bashing. But he might profitably raise questions about Reagan's plans and emphasize how they have no relation either to solving serious problems or to reality.

Budget deficits will not be wished away. Taxes will be raised, and programs that help people will be cut; it's inevitable. The question for voters to face is: Do you want Democrats or Republicans making those cuts and looking out for working people's interests?

As a political epitaph, Fritz Mondale could do worse than choose words that were favorites of his fellow Minnesotan who also had the bad luck to run in a non-Democratic year. Hubert Humphrey said: "The moral test of government is how it treats those who are in the dawn of life, the children; those who are in the twilight of life, the aged; and those who are in the shadows of life, the sick, the needy, and the handicapped."

November

Nov. 6 . . . Ronald Reagan re-elected in a landslide; wins 58.4% of vote, 525 electoral votes to 13, all states but Minnesota plus the District of Columbia. Democrats retain control of House, gain two Senate seats.

You don't have to be a militant feminist to be angry at the sexist smut, not just snickered in the locker room, but printed and openly available for purchase on buttons at Republican rallies, this fall. The question most frequently asked, always by men, of this itinerant political correspondent has been: What about Ferraro—has she hurt or helped?

Shrewd pol that she is, Geraldine Ferraro understands that a lot of people, many of whom don't agree with her on more than a few issues, are rooting for her To Do Well, whatever exactly that means. Ferraro hummed a few emotional bars on Phil Donahue's show when, in referring to her vice-presidential debate with George Bush, she said she understood that "I wasn't standing there for me alone. I was standing there for a lot of women in America who were saying: 'Oh God, I just don't want her to make a mistake.'"

In this campaign, without once publicly resorting to self-pity, Geraldine Ferraro has taken more scrutiny and slams than any vice-presidential candidate in recent history. Would that Spiro Agnew had been examined one-tenth as closely. She has been asked by people, so unobservant that they ignore the gutty fortitude with which she has borne all the vicious published rumors, whether she is tough enough to "push the button." She's a very tough lady.

* * * * *

Boston—Surrounded by Reagan Democrats, including former Massachusetts Governor Ed King and former Boston Mayor John Collins, and liberally quoting the revered John F. Kennedy, Ronald Reagan took the cheers of thousands here on the last Thursday of his last campaign. That the Republican conservative incumbent at this late hour boldly invaded the opposition's stronghold—the only commonwealth to have voted for every Democratic ticket from Kennedy-Johnson to Carter-Mondale—is more telling than all the polls, published or unpublished. Reagan is on the verge of a landslide victory. But, unlike 1980, it is to be a landslide without a mandate.

While most press criticism has fixed on the shortcomings of the Mondale organization, the 1984 Reagan effort may well turn out to be a campaign masterpiece and a political disaster. The Reagan campaign effectively submerged any ideas for a 1985 agenda or vision of where, specifically, Reagan would seek to lead the nation in a second term. The 1984 Reagan campaign has been more than disingenuous, it has been a disservice to the president. To win legislative support, Reagan, more than most chief executives, has relied on voters' validation of his program rather than on personal persuasion. That will be tough to do in 1985.

In 1981, there were no surprises for those who had listened to Reagan in 1980. As president, he used the momentum from his landslide to set about doing what he had said he would do: cutting the size, scope, and spending of government, doubling the defense budget, and cutting taxes by a third. This year he simply promised more of the same.

Now shattered is the national consensus on defense budgets which candidate Reagan helped forge in 1980. Even the president's painless New Patriotism—doubling the defense budget and then not paying for it by cutting everybody's taxes by one quarter—is in some trouble. Americans now believe the Pentagon wastes their money, that defense cuts can and must be made.

When the polls close on Tuesday, November 6, Ronald Reagan will become a political lame duck who will never again run for public office. In Washington, the perception of power frequently is power. Thanks to the Twenty-second Amendment, which limits presidents to two terms—the posthumous vengeance on the memory of FDR by some petty men who could not defeat our only four-term president in life—the current president's perceived power will be diminished.

In Ronald Reagan's last campaign, he ran once again against the past, making the 1984 vote a referendum on the 1980 results. The electorate's ratification, next Tuesday, of their 1980 choice of Ronald Reagan's America over Jimmy Carter's America could produce a 1984 landslide. But there will be no mandate for 1985: It could be a long four years.

* * * * *

Before eleven P.M. on the night of October 22, 1984, a full two weeks before the first voters would even cast their ballots on election day, the leadership of the Mondale-Ferraro campaign was told, by their own pollster, that the campaign was over, that Reagan had won.

Peter Hart is one of the truly respected professionals in American politics. One of the reasons you don't see him quoted as much as some other pollsters is because Hart is old-fashioned: he believes his first loyalty is to the candidate for whom he's working. He's notoriously tight-lipped about any numbers. It's been said of Peter Hart, that he wouldn't tell you if your coat was on fire. But he talked the other day, the election behind him, about when he as Fritz Mondale's pollster knew the game was over. It was the night after the second presidential debate. On the day of the debate, Peter Hart's polling showed Mondale trailing the president by just eleven percentage points—52 percent to 41 percent. And the Reagan polls had it just about the same. Both sides knew that the debate could change the race. And it did. Just twenty-four hours later, Hart's numbers had changed. Reagan had climbed to 57 percent and Mondale had slipped to 37 percent—a twenty-point margin. On the night of October 22, 1984, Peter Hart had the unpleasant task of telling Mondale's campaign manager that Fritz Mondale would not be elected president of the United States.

* * * * *

Back when he was Republican national chairman, Bill Brock became concerned because too many of his party's candidates were winning fewer than one out of ten black votes. He concluded, logically, that Republicans were doing something wrong; he set about trying to change the party's appearance, its approach and its message to black voters.

Contrast that with the attitude of a number of today's Democrats. Confronted with the bad news that their presidential ticket won only three out of ten white male votes Tuesday, they find no fault with their ideas or themselves. Instead, they exhibit a marked preference for blaming the

" I'M A REGISTERED DEMOCRAT ... BUT I'VE GOT A SECRET PLAN TO VOTE REPUBLICAN ! "

results on terminal macho-ness in the population, or racial polarization. As an explanation or excuse, that may be convenient, but it is wrong.

For these analysts, the villain of the piece in 1984 turns out to be a constituency: white male voters, who comprise about 45 percent of the nation's electorate, a rather sizable group to dismiss as misanthropic or otherwise unfit for even a walk-on role in the Democrats' morality play.

This latest excuse gets a strong dissent from Arkansas Democratic Senator Dale Bumpers who has been winning statewide elections (and the votes of white males) for fifteen years. Bumpers rejects the macho/racist explanation: "Americans, male as well as female, are not meaner than a one-eyed water moccasin. People do not want to be polarized. And we cannot blame our political failures on the voters."

Bumpers' reading is supported by this year's Senate campaign in neighboring Mississippi, where incumbent Thad Cochran became the first homestate Republican since Reconstruction to win a majority of the vote. Both Cochran and his respected opponent, former Democratic Governor William Winter, ran honorable campaigns free of the ugly racial politics that for so long sullied their state.

Americans have, in the past twenty years, made historic progress in overcoming centuries of segregation and discrimination, and worse. Civil rights laws enacted over the insensitive and unthinking opposition of Ronald Reagan and others have made a great and positive difference.

Of course, prejudice, as indicated by Jesse Helms's successful North Carolina Senate campaign, remains—sadly—a factor in American politics. But this should not prevent Democrats from confronting reality.

The Democratic party's candidates have suffered landslide defeats in three of the last four presidential elections, but not because the electorate is mean-spirited or vengeful. Democrats have lost because what they have stood for in those elections—and in between—has not been particularly relevant, believable or practical to a majority of American voters. Candidates who blame their problems on the intellectual or moral shortcomings of the voters deserve defeat. And usually get what they deserve.

＊　＊　＊　＊　＊

Whenever a new president is elected, especially when he replaces an administration of the opposite party as Ronald Reagan did four years ago in 1980, we more or less expect that new president to discover that the mess in Washington is worse than even he had imagined.

Such a discovery permits the new president to take more drastic and dramatic action than he had proposed during the campaign. But reelected presidents are different. Because they have already been president, and presumably are enough in charge of things to be reelected, they are not allowed to discover suddenly that the federal government is now out of parachutes or petty cash. Nevertheless, this week, only a few days after his historic landslide victory, President Reagan seems to be discovering that unlike adolescent pimples, the federal deficit is something we will not simply grow our way out of. And the deficit is now discovered to be a lot bigger than it was only one week ago. That just won't do. New presidents can discover, but reelected presidents don't have the same kind of latitude.

Back when the Republicans were in what seemed to be a permanent congressional minority, championing the balanced-budget amendment, just like voting against any increases in the federal debt ceiling, was fun politics with which to torment the governing majority party. But after converting to supply-side economics, which essentially ignores deficits in favor of economic growth, Republicans and the White House would do well to follow the consistent leadership of Representative Jack Kemp who, to his credit, refuses to indulge in the frivolous deceit of simultaneously advocating tax cuts and a balanced-budget amendment.

*   *   *   *   *

All who pretend to be fair-minded are obliged to admire the resilience and resourcefulness of Democrats, still reeling from yet another pasting at the polls. Prominent Democrats, cheerfully ignoring the carnage in their ranks, crow that Ronald Reagan next January will have fewer members of his party in the House of Representatives than any elected or reelected president since Grover Cleveland. See, exult the Democrats, our party is in good shape where it counts most—at the local level.

What these "Norman Vincent Peale" Democrats choose to overlook is that any political party that remains noncompetitive at the national level for a generation or more finds itself eventually without either philosophical cohesiveness or a farm system of talented, young candidates eager to run for office.

Consider the dilemma of a Democratic House candidate in

recent presidential years. Being a good partisan, you hope your party's nominee wins the White House. You also hope the national ticket gives you a boost in your own district. But for most Democratic House candidates over the past twenty years, that has been a futile hope. In 1968, Hubert Humphrey came within an eyelash of winning the presidency, but was able to carry only 160 House districts. In 1980, Jimmy Carter carried only 127 districts; and in that memorable year, 1972, George McGovern defeated Richard Nixon in only 57 districts out of 435. In each of these three presidential elections, 243 House Democrats still managed to win election—on their own, despite the drag at the top of the ticket.

The presidential issues—the economy, national defense, the proper role of the federal government—intrude upon House campaigns. GOP House candidates have generally seen political advantage for themselves in echoing the positions and the rhetoric of their presidential nominee on national issues. Such public agreement among Republican candidates encourages party unity before the election and party unity after.

For Democrats, the opposite case has prevailed: House candidates, concerned about their own elections, have chosen not to share the same platform—either philosophically or sometimes even physically—with their national running mates. They have had to run and win on their own, which has frequently meant an emphasis on different issues in different districts and, almost always, on independence from the national party.

As the pro-politics and pro-government party, the Democrats have been able to attract as candidates a disproportionate share of those college graduates who are energetic, articulate, and aggressive. In a number of strongly Republican congressional districts, Democratic representatives—such as Les AuCoin in Oregon, Matt McHugh in New York, and Tim Wirth in Colorado—have been able to win because they are superior politically to anyone the Republicans, with all their megabucks and state-of-the-art machinery, have been able to recruit to run against them.

But the Democratic farm system of youthful talent shows

signs of depletion. Ronald Reagan won three out of five votes of those under the age of thirty, which—if the pattern holds—can only be bad for the Democrats. The Democrats have been the beneficiaries of the legacy of Adlai Stevenson and John F. Kennedy, whose careers inspired hundreds of candidates, and of the stupidity of Richard Nixon and Spiro Agnew, whose angry attacks on college anti-war protesters helped to drive a whole generation of potential candidates away from the Republicans. Nixon and Agnew made it almost impossible, because of peer pressure, for young people to be Republicans.

But that, too, could be changing as Democratic idealism and optimism run dry. Without unity and talent, no party can long prosper.